W9-AEA-560

Founders of Christian Movements

CONTRIBUTORS TO THIS VOLUME

A. J. W. Myers
Head of Department of Religious Education
Hartford School of Religious Education

Frank Glenn Lankard
Dean, Brothers College
Drew University

G. Walter Fiske
Emeritus Professor of Practical Theology
Oberlin Graduate School of Theology

Georgia Harkness
Professor of Applied Theology
Garrett Biblical Institute

Lois R. Robison
Author
Bronxville, N. Y.

W. D. Schermerhorn
Emeritus Professor of Church History
Garrett Biblical Institute

Henry H. Meyer
Professor of Religious Education
School of Theology, Boston University

Lowell B. Hazzard
Pastor, Union Methodist Church
Quincy, Illinois

James V. Thompson
Chairman, Division of Religious Education
Drew University

Eva Jean Wrather
Author
Nashville, Tenn.

Laura H. Wild
Emeritus Professor of Biblical Literature
Mt. Holyoke College

Thomas R. Kelly
Associate Professor of Philosophy
Haverford College

John W. Prince
Pastor, Methodist Church
Clinton, Connecticut

Founders of Christian Movements

Edited by
PHILIP HENRY LOTZ

Essay Index Reprint Series

BOOKS FOR LIBRARIES PRESS
FREEPORT, NEW YORK

Originally published as Volume III of the
Creative Personalities Series

Reprinted 1970 by arrangement with Association Press

STANDARD BOOK NUMBER:
8369-1672-7

LIBRARY OF CONGRESS CATALOG CARD NUMBER:
71-111843

PRINTED IN THE UNITED STATES OF AMERICA

Introduction

I

"GREAT men need not that we praise them; the need is ours that we know them."[1] The fifteen men whose lives and achievements are described in this little volume begin with the Apostle Paul in the first Christian century and conclude with Walter Rauschenbusch and William Booth in the twentieth century. Each one was the founder of a Christian movement or communion and has influenced hosts of people. Though they lived in different centuries, spoke different languages, and belonged to different races and nations, their loyalty to the lowly Nazarene was common to all.

"The great movements in human history, its great epochs have been marked by the rise of some strong personality. Someone has well said that it is the man with a great conviction that has changed the course of history."[2] St. Paul represents Christianity as a missionary religion; Martin Luther was the genius of the Protestant Reformation; John Wesley incarnated the spirit of the Evangelical Revival and the Wesleyan movement; Robert Raikes was the founder of the Sunday-school movement; and William Booth founded the Salvation Army, world-wide in extent. Truly, "personality constitutes the most proper category for divine revelation."[3]

Here one finds William Ellery Channing, one of the great ethical and religious leaders of New England. He never learned to play. He was not blessed with a strong and healthy body. Yet

[1] Arthur C. McGiffert.

[2] James E. Freeman.

[3] James Muilenberg.

he believed in "the perfectibility of man." Founder of Unitarianism, that church still accepts his statement of belief:

The Fatherhood of God
The Brotherhood of Man
The Leadership of Jesus
Salvation by Character and the
Continued progress of Man, upward.

George Fox was the founder of the Society of Friends, often called Quakers. He was the great prophet of the "Light Within." He found the religious leaders of his day "hollow, empty casks." He refused to take an oath; he was deprived of his citizenship; he was cast into prison repeatedly under indescribable conditions. Today there is no name spoken with greater respect than that of the Society of Friends.

Alexander Campbell was the spiritual father of the Disciples of Christ, sometimes called Campbellites. His formal college training was confined to a single year, yet he later founded a college. He became a gentleman farmer, an editor, writer, preacher, debater, college teacher and president, and delegate to a constitutional convention. He was a commanding public speaker. He held the doctrine of "Believers' Immersion," and was an apostle of the unity and purity of the church.

Horace Bushnell called himself "One of God's experimenters." He invented a furnace, was an engineer who promoted roads and parks, an athlete, and one of the founders of the Beethoven Society at Yale. He was the pioneer apostle of Christian Nurture or Religious Education. His major philosophy was stated in these words: "The child is to grow up a Christian and never to know itself as being otherwise."

John Calvin has been called "the man with the iron will." Calvinism has often been synonymous with predestination. At fourteen he entered the University of Paris. Later he was driven from both Paris and Geneva, though he was recalled to Geneva. He persecuted the heretics: Gruet was beheaded and Servetus was burned at the stake.

Walter Rauschenbusch was the prophet of the "Social Gospel."

He was a scholar, teacher, minister, preacher, theologian, historian, and social worker. In his first charge in New York City he received the meager salary of $600. In spite of being almost totally deaf, he was a great teacher. From 1914 to 1918 he wore black crêpe on his sleeve to indicate his hatred for war. His half dozen great books profoundly influenced the interpretation of Christianity.

Other creative personalities described are St. Francis of Assisi, founder of the Franciscan Order; St. Benedict, founder of Western Monasticism; Ignatius Loyola, author of *A Spiritual Manual of Arms;* and Ludwig von Zinzendorf, the most distinguished of the Moravian Brethren.

II

The foregoing paragraphs are merely snapshots of the men whom history pronounces creative personalities. In this third volume by that name, nationally known ministers, teachers, writers, and religious educators have collaborated with the editor to tell the stories of these great pioneers, pathfinders, and prophets, who initiated and stamped with their imprint some of the greatest movements in history. Desirable ideas, ideals, attitudes, and habits have been dramatized in terms of dynamic human personality.

The *Creative Personalities* series is designed primarily for young people and leaders of young people though it will prove of equal interest and value to those who enjoy high adventure. It has been our aim to provide unhackneyed biographical teaching material for the church school, the club, the home, and classes in character education and citizenship, and readily available and usable material for public addresses.

Each sketch is written briefly, interestingly, and to the point. Questions for discussion and supplementary reading suggestions are attached and should be provoking. The constant goal of the entire series has been to provide interesting, practical, and dynamic material for young people of the upper high-school and lower college level of thought and experience.

Two volumes in this series have already been published: *Voca-*

tions and Professions, and *Women Leaders.* Other volumes now in preparation will deal with:

Nationalities and Races
Founders of Religions and Philosophical and Ethical Systems
Negro Geniuses
Distinguished American Jews

PHILIP HENRY LOTZ

Wenona, Illinois.
December, 1940.

Contents

Robert Raikes

by

A. J. W. Myers

Head of Department of Religious Education
Hartford School of Religious Education

RAGGED CHILDREN

"Do THESE miserable mobs of children belong to this part of the town?"

"Sir, you should see this place on Sunday! The pin factories and other shops are shut then, and the noise and riot, the cursing and swearing, make this place a hell. There is no self restraint."

"Do the parents not care?"

"They are totally abandoned themselves, and ignorant."

"What of the church?"

"We have a good rector. He has got some to go to school. But what can be done with this rabble on Sunday?"

The Stranger says that one word kept throbbing in his mind—the little word "Try, try, try." A thought struck him. Turning again to the woman, he asked, "Are there any decent, well-disposed women in the neighborhood, who keep 'kitchen' or 'dame' schools for teaching reading?"

"Yes, indeed. Three or four such," and she pointed out where they lived.

The Stranger called on the rector and then went to the four teachers, and a dialogue like this ensued, after the general opening polite conversation:

"If you were paid for it, would you undertake to teach some of these heathen from the streets every Sunday?"

"What age children? Some from the streets are too big to handle."

"We would enroll only those six to twelve or perhaps fourteen years of age."

"What would I teach them?"

"Well, reading, the Bible, and the catechism. *Vice is preventable. Begin with the child.*"

"What hours?"

"Those can be agreed on. Suppose we start with having them from ten to twelve in the morning, have them come back at one for a few minutes, then go to church, and repeat the catechism till, say, five thirty. I will pay one shilling a Sunday."

"Yes, I'd like to try. Will there be any rules or any help? Some of these will be tough characters."

"We will make one rule. Any who come must have clean hands and face, and hair combed. Doubtless they cannot afford good clothes, but if they can be on the street they can come to school.

"As for moral support, the rector promises to try to get them to come, and he and I will visit every Sunday. We will have little gifts to encourage those who do well."

RAGGED SCHOOLS

So the work began. Meeting on Sundays, they were called "Sunday Schools." The stranger was none other than Robert Raikes. This was his great experiment. The first Sunday school was in Soot, or Sooty, Alley! Raikes sometimes referred to these schools as "My little project for civilizing the rising generation of the poor."[1]

"This, sir, was the commencement of the plan," concluded Raikes in his reply to a letter of inquiry from Colonel Townley to the Mayor of Gloucester![2] Harris gives the date as 1780,[3] and Lloyd, 1781 or

---

[1] J. B. *Robert Raikes: His Sunday Schools and His Friends.* Philadelphia, American Baptist Publication Society, 1895, p. 66. This book has no author's name, but the preface is signed J. B. John Carroll Power, in his book, *The Rise and Progress of Sunday Schools,* p. 47, says the author evidently "was the Rev. Joseph Belcher, D.D. He was a native of England and died in Philadelphia in the year 1860 at an advanced age."

[2] The same, p. 21.

[3] Harris, J. Henry. *The Story of Robert Raikes for the Young.* Philadelphia, Union Press, 1900, p. 55.

early 1782.[4] In another place, Harris says[5] November 4, 1783, but as this was the date Raikes' letter appeared in the *Gloucester Journal,* the beginning must have been earlier. The date is probably 1780 or 1781.

Mr. Raikes visited all the homes and talked to the parents. He was constantly at the Sunday schools and churches. He had gifts of Bibles or other little books, combs, shoes, or other articles of clothing for those who did well. He stated some of the aims of the school as follows:

"to be kind and good-natured to each other; not to provoke one another; to be dutiful to their parents; not to offend God by cursing and swearing; and such little plain precepts as all may comprehend. . . . Often have I given them kind admonitions, which I always do in the mildest and gentlest manner partly because, when quarrels have arisen, the transgressor is compelled to ask pardon, and the offended is enjoined to forgive. The kindness that must arise to all from a kind, good-natured behavior, is often inculcated."[6]

Boys only were admitted at first, partly because they were the toughest of street arabs. After a few years, girls were enrolled also, and some of them were worse than the boys.

Raikes published a little textbook, which he called *Redinmadesy* (reading made easy), for these schools.[7]

It is easy to understand how the children, accustomed to brutal treatment, responded to kindness, and how "Bobby Wild Goose"[8] would be one of the politest names these factory slum savages called Raikes. Raikes was amazed at their devotion to him, and also how many showed eagerness to learn. So he discovered "genius and innate good dispositions among the little multitude." And he added this striking and famous sentence: "It is botanizing in human

[4] Lloyd, W. F. *Sketch of the Life of Robert Raikes, Esq., and the History of Sunday Schools.* New York, Hunt & Eaton, 1891, p. 11.

[5] Gregory, Alfred. *Robert Raikes: Journalist and Philanthropist.* London, Hodder & Stoughton, 1881, p. 286.

[6] J. B. *Robert Raikes, His Sunday Schools and His Friends,* pp. 25, 26, and 33.

[7] *The Development of the Sunday School, 1780-1905.* Boston, International Sunday School Association, p. 4.

[8] Harris, J. Henry. *Robert Raikes, the Man and His Work.* New York, Dutton, 1899, p. 291.

nature."[9] Some pupils were given additional time on weekdays, for which the teachers received one or two shillings extra.

And what a New Year's day that was in 1795 for these banditti of the streets. "I have invited all my Sunday School children to dine with me on beef and plum pudding. I wish you could step in and see. . . ."[10] What a sight it must have been! Raikes, the dandy, loved this rabble. That is what always counts.

RESULTS

Good results of the Sunday schools were immediately apparent. In a letter, Raikes wrote:

"A woman who lived in a lane where I had fixed a school, told me some time ago, that the place was quite a heaven upon Sundays compared with what it used to be. . . . But what is yet more extraordinary, within this month these little ragamuffins have in great numbers taken it into their heads to frequent the early morning prayers, which are held every morning at the cathedral at seven o'clock. I believe there were near fifty this morning."[11]

He quotes the testimony of Mr. Church, a considerable manufacturer of hemp and flax, who employs great numbers of these children. Mr. Church, who was probably one of the most humane of employers, reveals incidentally the attitude of the upper class to the "hands" employed. This is his reply:

"Sir," said he, "the change could not have been more extraordinary, in my opinion, had they been transformed from the shape of wolves and tigers to that of men. In temper, disposition, and manners, they could hardly be said to differ from the brute creation. But since the establishment of the Sunday Schools, they have seemed anxious to show that they are not the ignorant, illiterate creatures they were before. . . . In short, I never conceived that a reformation so singular could have been effected amongst the set of untutored beings I employ."[12]

Inquiries poured in. The *Gentleman's Magazine,* which had a

[9] J. B. *Robert Raikes, His Sunday Schools and His Friends,* p. 26.
[10] Harris, *Story of Robert Raikes for the Young,* p. 78.
[11] J. B. *Robert Raikes, His Sunday Schools and His Friends,* p. 24.
[12] The same, pp. 33-34.

large circulation among influential people, published one of these letters from which quotations have been made. The result was an enormous increase of Sunday schools.

THE CHURCHES AND SUNDAY SCHOOLS

As has been indicated, some ministers worked in Sunday schools from the first: Wesley was enthusiastic about them and promoted them. In his *Journal,* July 18, 1784, he says he was at Bingley Church, where there were 240 children in Sunday school. At Bolton he found 550 children with 80 masters, none of whom were paid. Queen Charlotte, Hanna More, Wilberforce, and others were interested. In four years, 250,000 were enrolled, and the number was growing rapidly. Sabbath-evening schools became popular in Scotland, and adult schools in Wales.

But many ministers, bishops, and lay people opposed because of desecration of the Sabbath; because ministers should teach the parents, and parents their own children; because the lower classes should not be taught above their station; and because results might lead to the overturn of social classes and the government. Many opposed them bitterly, calling them works of the devil.

Some ministers wanted all to attend the church service twice a day. Robert Raikes writes,

"Their attending the service of the church once a day, has to me seemed sufficient, for their time may be spent more profitably, perhaps, in receiving instruction, than in being present at a long discourse, which their minds are not yet able to comprehend."[13]

ORGANIZATION

William Fox, born near Gloucester in the same year as Raikes, 1736, the youngest of eight children, made a fortune by his own efforts. He was a devout member of the church and greatly interested in helping those in need. After buying Clapton manor, in his native village, his first attempt was "to clothe comfortably all the poor people in the village—men, women, and children. He next set up a weekday school for the free instruction of all who were

[13] J. B. *Robert Raikes, His Sunday Schools and His Friends,* p. 68.

willing to attend it." His wish was "that every poor person in the Kingdom might be able to read the Bible."[14]

This scheme for universal education among the poor was too ambitious without government action. Then Fox heard of the Sunday schools and entered into correspondence with Raikes. Fox and interested friends became enthusiastic, and as a result, "the *First Sunday School Society ever known was organized in the City of London on the seventh day of September,* A. D. 1785."[15] The name finally decided on was "The Society For Promoting Sunday Schools Throughout the British Dominions," and it was popularly known as "The Sunday School Society."

There is no evidence that Raikes ever thought of the Sunday school becoming a national or world movement, but without this wider outlook and organization it would likely have disappeared when the immediate need was met. This is a good example of how different minds contribute to the success of a cause.

THE DAY SCHOOL AND THE SUNDAY SCHOOL

The church owes much to the public school. The public school owes much to the Sunday school. This is what Wade says in his *History of the Middle and Working Classes:*

"Before their establishment, education was at a very low ebb, even among the middle orders, as may be seen by the writing and spelling of respectable tradesmen of that period. The improvement in the education of the working classes gave an impulse to the education of the classes immediately above them."[16]

Besides, these "Ragged," or Sunday, schools gave a great impetus to the whole idea of public education for all classes.

ROBERT RAIKES

And who is Robert Raikes? He belonged to an old Yorkshire family.[17] His father was a prosperous printer, and publisher of the *Gloucester Journal.* He left his son ample means and a good busi-

[14] Power, John C. *The Rise and Progress of Sunday Schools, a Biography of Robert Raikes and William Fox.* New York, Sheldon & Co., 1871, p. 62.

[15] Power, *Rise and Progress of Sunday Schools,* p. 87.

[16] J. B. *Robert Raikes, His Sunday Schools and His Friends,* p. 88.

[17] Power, *Rise and Progress of Sunday Schools,* pp. 28-31.

ness. Robert was born in Gloucester, England, on September 14, 1736. His mother was much younger than her husband and was a lovely character. All five sons and a daughter were well educated and prosperous, worthy citizens: Thomas became governor of the Bank of England;[18] Robert was not only editor of a paper, but, his daughter says, he "wrote French fluently, and was a first-rate geographer."[19]

Raikes moved in fashionable society, as did his wife. One of her brothers was General Sir Thomas Trigge, and another was an admiral.[20] Raikes was quite domestic and lived happily with his wife and, as he said, "six excellent daughters and two lovely sons."[21]

Some claim that he had many weaknesses. He was said to have been vain and ostentatious; at times harsh if not cruel with the children; and, like most other good people of his time, never dreamed of improving factory conditions and wages. They were content if "while the poor remain destitute of the comforts of this life, they may not be altogether unacquainted with that which is to come."

> "Let Poverty or want be what it will,
> It does proceed from God; therefore's no ill,"

sang Stephen Duck.[22]

But in most of these attitudes Raikes was a child of his time. It is all the more to his credit that he rose above personal limitations and social conditions to meet human needs.

He early became interested in the deplorable conditions of the people in Gloucester jail and did much to provide them with the necessities of life, some little educational opportunities, and even some work. He also opposed the cruel sport of cockfighting and was a strong advocate of temperance.

It is not surprising, then, that when he saw the condition of the mill children on the streets on Sunday, he should feel the urge to try to do something about it. Because of the need, the good results,

---

[18] Harris, *Story of Robert Raikes for the Young*, pp. 25-37.

[19] Caroline Weller-Ladbroke's letter, quoted in Harris, *Robert Raikes, the Man and His Work*, p. 209.

[20] Harris, *Story of Robert Raikes for the Young*, pp. 32-33.

[21] Harris, *Robert Raikes, the Man and His Work*, p. 185.

[22] "On Poverty," 1728.

and the publicity given to the schools through magazines and other publications, the idea spread with enormous rapidity in spite of opposition.

No movement like this is the work of one person. Sunday schools had existed before this time in various places. Many people worked wholeheartedly with Raikes and, like William Fox, helped extend it far beyond the original purpose. A very great deal of credit must be given to Rev. Thomas Stock and especially to the women teachers who had the grace and courage to admit this dirty, ragged, swearing, ill-mannered rabble into their houses.

HIS MONUMENT

Raikes died in his house in Bell Lane, Gloucester, England, on April 5, 1811, at the age of seventy-five and is buried in "the ancient church of St. Mary de Crypt."[23] His grave was marked by a simple slab of marble, two feet square, in a dark corner, and no mention is made on it of his founding the Sunday school.[24]

It often happens that a prophet is not recognized in his own time, nor the value of his work appreciated. But a century later, in 1880, a statue was erected to him on the Thames Embankment, one of the most prominent sites in the great city of London. Where he lived in Gloucester is now a place of pilgrimage for people from all over the world.

But his real monument is the vast Sunday school population throughout the whole world. The figures are astonishing—more than thirty million, with more than three million teachers and officers! Compared with this, monuments of brass or marble are insignificant.

For Discussion

1. Compare the work and influence of Robert Raikes and of, say, Hitler. Discuss this statement, "A good life enhances the life of every other person."
2. Study social conditions in 1780 and now, comparing: care of children; jails; factory conditions, hours of work, and pay; drink; and so on.

---

[23] Lloyd, *Sketch of the Life of Robert Raikes*, p. 70.
[24] Harris, *Story of Robert Raikes for the Young*, p. 5.

3. Raikes helped people in need—the people in jail, the ragged children. How did this habit of doing what he could at once influence his life? What are some urgent human needs today?
4. Religious education includes children and youth and men and women. Raikes did great work in his own day. What can the young people do in your church today? Work out your statement of needs and of how the young people can help.
5. Compare the origin of the Sunday school and of the Vacation Church School. Are there Vacation Church Schools where young people can help or areas nearby where these schools should be started?

For Further Reading

J. B. *Robert Raikes: His Sunday Schools and His Friends.* Philadelphia, American Baptist Publication Society, 1859.

Gregory, Alfred. *Robert Raikes: Journalist and Philanthropist.* London, Hodder & Stoughton, 1881.

Harris, J. Henry. *Robert Raikes, the Man and His Work.* New York, Dutton, 1899.

Harris, J. Henry. *The Story of Robert Raikes for the Young.* Philadelphia, Union Press, 1900.

Hayes, Ernest Henry. *Raikes the Pioneer: Founder of Sunday Schools.* London, National Sunday School Union, 1930.

Lloyd, W. F. *Sketch of the Life of Robert Raikes, Esq., and of the History of Sunday Schools.* New York, Hunt & Eaton, 1891.

Power, John C. *The Rise and Progress of Sunday Schools, a Biography of Robert Raikes and William Fox.* New York, Sheldon & Co., 1871.

The Development of the Sunday School, 1780-1905. Boston, The International Sunday School Association, 1905.

William Booth

by

Frank Glenn Lankard
Dean, Brothers College
Drew University

"Christ for me! Be that your motto! Be that your battle cry! Be that your war note! Be that your consolation! Be that your plea when asking mercy of God, your end when offering it to man, your hope when encircled by darkness, your triumph and victory when attacked and overcome by death! Christ for me! Your General assures you of success and a glorious reward! Your crown is already held out! Then why delay? Why doubt? Onward! Onward! Onward!"[1] It was with these sincere and passionate words that General William Booth led the movement known as the Salvation Army.

At Christmas time, if at no other season of the year, when we hurry along the city streets bent on our Christmas shopping, we see a man or woman in uniform, ringing a small bell and cheerfully asking for a contribution to the big black kettle that hangs suspended from a tripod. Little do we realize, perhaps, that the guardian of the black kettle belongs to a movement that is widespread, has attracted world-wide attention, has been the victim of fierce opposition, has been slandered, misrepresented, ridiculed, misunderstood, held in contempt, but has been a ray of light in dark places, nevertheless, to thousands of men and women who needed the touch of a friendly and loving hand.

It is a truism that great movements owe their origin and sustaining enthusiasms to one or more creative personalities, and the Sal-

[1] Booth-Tucker, Frederick. *William Booth, the General of the Salvation Army.* The Salvation Army Printing and Publishing Company, New York, 1898, p. 1.

vation Army is no exception. Its founder and first great leader was General William Booth, and to understand the movement that he led, we ought to know something of the man himself and the conditions of life that led to the movement he initiated. William Booth first saw the light of day on April 10, 1829, in a little suburb of Nottingham, England.

CONDITIONS IN ENGLAND

The period in which Booth lived was marked by economic and social distress. The bad effects of the Napoleonic wars had not yet been forgotten; unemployed men wandered through the streets of England in search of work; high prices prevailed as a result of crop failures, the corn law, and the greed of the selfish land owners. In his early and impressionable years, he was familiar with murders, highway robbery, riots and insurrections, drunken crowds, the sacking of baker shops, and the misery and destitution that filled the streets of British towns with infuriated mobs shouting for food until the authorities were compelled to read the Riot Act. Thousands of people were compelled to seek relief at the hands of the government.

BOYHOOD AND FORMATIVE INFLUENCES

The father of William Booth was nominally a church man but a hard, taciturn, and unemotional man. He was a builder by trade, who had earned and lost a fortune. William's mother, Mary Moss, was his father's second wife, a very beautiful woman of a warm, cheerful, and optimistic temperament. Of this union there were five children, the eldest a boy who died in childhood, the second a daughter, the third child the Evangelist himself, and the two remaining children girls.

Among his boyhood companions, William was the leader from the very first. He was known as "Willful Will," and is described as a carefree, hardheaded, and mischievous lad—a boy among boys. Fortunately for the lad, there was a tract of land not far from his home known as the "Meadows," which contained flowers, paths, woods, and a river, which furnished a pleasant contrast to the hard, poverty-stricken conditions of the village. William was like his father in that he possessed a strong will and like his mother in his sensitive appreciation of beauty and his love of nature.

As a boy, William was not deeply religious. At one time he felt the lack of religion, brought about it seems by the songs that he sang at the parish church and the influence of a religiously minded cousin. But, this feeling was short-lived. There was, however, one incident in his boyhood that brought him into contact with the Methodists. The parents of an only child who had died took a deep interest in William because he resembled their son. Through their kindness, William was taken to the Wesleyan Chapel, and there he gained the first real religious training of his life. Later, William's father suffered complete financial ruin, and within a year died of the strain. Just before his death, he seriously repented of his sinful life, and this repentance and the burial made a profound impression on William, who broke with the Church of England and began to spend much time with the Wesleyans. In the midst of the problems and worries of supporting his father's family and mastering his own business (pawnbroker), he began to take religion much more seriously.

In the political excitement of 1842, Booth sided with the Charterists, who sympathized with the poor, and thus Booth was regarded as a radical. So it came about that the young man had three interests: he wanted to be successful in business; he wished to be active in political reform; and he was seeking a more satisfying religious experience. At the age of fifteen, when he was but a shop assistant, he was converted. It consisted in making a total surrender of his whole being to God. He cast himself completely on God's pardon and gave himself up wholly to His Service with all his heart. So real was this experience to him that he says the hour, the place, and many of the particulars of the glorious transaction were indelibly recorded in his memory.

RELIGIOUS ACTIVITIES

There were two events following Booth's conversion that greatly influenced his future work. One was a remarkable religious awakening that swept the local society of which Booth was a member, which made the entire community religion conscious. The other was the vivid realization on the part of the young man that the religious principle was so applicable to the problems of the poor and desolate. The realization that religion has a mission to the poor and destitute of the earth came to have concrete reality in Booth's later plans.

The evangelistic fervor growing out of the local revival caused some of his friends to hold meetings in the poorer section of the town. William Booth, although stricken by illness, followed the effort closely, and upon his recovery took an active part in the work. The procedure was simple. The service began in the open air, and after a time proceeded to a cottage which had been borrowed for the purpose. On Sunday, the smaller groups were taken to the Chapel. We have here, in reality, the miniature Salvation Army.

In time, Booth yielded to the persuasion to become a local preacher, but refused to become a regular minister on the ground of ill health. During all of this time Booth was still supporting his father's family, from whom he received little or no encouragement, and many of the people of the church felt that he was going too far. His efforts were with the ragged group of society, and he was compelled to bring it in at the back door at the big Chapel for Sunday services.

At nineteen, William completed his term of apprenticeship, and, unable to secure work in Nottingham, he decided to go to London. He found London a great disappointment, particularly on the human side, and he was quick to notice that the lower level of society received no consideration. In London, Booth became a minister in the Methodist New Connection, and, securing a chapel in the East End of London, he carried on evangelistic work. The call to the regular ministry of the Methodist New Connection was not a dramatic summons but a steady growth. It was not only from Heaven but from humanity as well. In time, there were some unpleasant difficulties that led Booth to sever his relations with the Methodist New Connection. It was not an easy step to take with an empty purse, for by this time he had married, his wife was in poor health, and there were four small children to be cared for. But when the break came, Booth stepped out to do the work that he believed God had planned for him. The Wesleyan Conference in 1861 ruled that Booth could not hold meetings in their chapels. This act proved to be but one more step in forcing

Booth to serve the poverty groups not through one church but for all churches.

Not all of the churches, however, were closed to the Booths. It is only fair to say that the wife of William Booth was a very consecrated and competent woman who shared her husband's work to the full and proved to be of great help in it. At Walstall, England, a group of Methodists had constructed a beautiful chapel, but they could not get a congregation. The upper classes were too proud and the lower classes too hostile. Could Booth help? After trying one thing after another with little or no success, Booth decided to organize what became known as the "Hallelujah Band." It consisted of a group of former celebrities, prize-fighters, jail-birds, etc. This ill assortment of persons organized into a gospel band caught the local imagination, and a great crowd assembled and many were converted. The evangelistic effort proved to be a great success, but the remarkable success was turned into failure because the church leaders could not agree on the best methods of procedure. Both the experiment and the shortsightedness of the church leaders, which really turned success into failure, were vividly engraved on the memory of William Booth.

THE FOUNDING OF THE SALVATION ARMY

In 1865 the Booths again moved to London, where they had decided to make their home and serve the needy and destitute. London was being moved by a series of open-air and tent services, and Booth was invited to hold tent services in the East End, where he was very successful. The tent was destroyed by a storm, but the place of meeting only changed to a dance hall, then a wool warehouse, an old chapel, a stable, a penny gaff, a skittle alley, a beer house, the old Effingham Theatre, etc. But, in spite of all vicissitudes, the movement continued to grow.

The class of people to whom Booth was ministering was the very lowest and poorest. Most of his believers had never heard of the love of God before in their lives, and they poured out their hearts in repentance. What should his followers be called? Where should they go? Booth did not care to form a new religious sect, but he was unable to get his followers to find a home in the other churches. Three factors militated against such an end. First, the new converts would not go when sent; second, they were not welcomed by the other churches; and third, Booth really needed the best of them for furthering his evangelistic efforts in London's East End. The new converts, however, for lack of work and a church home, were "backsliding" rapidly. Some organization and rallying slogans were imperative. At first, Booth called his movement the East London Revival, then the East London Christian Mission, the Christian Mission, the Volunteer Army, and last, the Salvation Army.

The creation and final organization of the Salvation Army were the result of a process of growth. Booth believed that his converts could become evangelists like himself, and stations were established as centers of worship, in order that the teaching could go on more rapidly. A yearly Conference of the evangelists was provided for, in order that they might discuss their mutual problems and progress. The Conference at first was quite democratic, but theological differences soon brought about a Council of War under the dictatorship of William Booth.

There were many weaknesses or points of probable failure in the Christian Mission. It grew so rapidly that it was hard to control. The responsibility for its success or failure was too great for one family. Wealthy men were able to determine the activities of certain stations by the size of their gifts. There was a natural tendency for each leader of a station to create and set forth his beliefs and teachings rather than those of the founder. Many people were writing and speaking in a vein quite antagonistic to the movement. The average onlooker raised questions of financial integrity. Both William Booth and his wife were not strong physically, and their frail health was not equal to the many problems.

In 1878, William Booth, cognizant of the difficulties and weaknesses, organized the Salvation Army, in order to have an effective control of his followers. The organization followed the lines employed by the English military and naval systems, employing such terms and offices as General, Lieutenant, Council of War, War Congress, Captain, Army, etc. A flag, uniform, titles, and brass bands all became a part of the new system.

Good results were obvious from the beginning. Within a year, fifty stations were organized and eighty-eight evangelists were at work. The bitter criticisms gave way to more favorable written and spoken comments. Religious services were held in almost every conceivable place—circuses, theatres, music halls, and in the open air.

THE WORK OF THE ARMY

The Salvation Army began to publish a newspaper known as the *War Cry*. It proved to be a happy medium for making known the progress and success of the fight against sin and poverty.

By 1880, there was a demand for Army corps in Australia, the United States, and Canada. Soon the work of the Army spread to France, Sweden, India, New Zealand, and South Africa. Truly, it has become universal in its influence.

Beyond question, the Salvation Army has had real success. One reason is that it aimed at great and noble goals. It showed its ability to deal with the problems of sin-cursed men throughout the world. A second reason was the ability and stamina gained from a stream of opposition that constantly caused the Army to gird itself for greater accomplishments. We need to remember that the movement was organized into an army, and the opposition that came from brothels, houses of drink and prostitution, ruffians, mobs, and hostile police only made it seem like a real war. Everything helped to capture the imagination, and certainly the fire had taken the fuel.

In 1885, the Purity Crusade began. It was a crusade against white slavery and houses of prostitution. It aimed at better conditions for troubled, fallen women, and it rendered significant service.

As time went on, General Booth decided to have the Army give more attention to social reform as a supplement to its religious work. His heart went out to those who had no capital or income of their own and to those who had difficulty in obtaining the regulation allowances of food that the law prescribed.

The scheme that Booth worked out to aid these defenseless groups of humanity consisted of ten expedients: (1) the city colony; (2) the farm colony; (3) the oversea colony; (4) the household salvage brigade; (5) the rescue homes for the fallen women; (6) deliverances for the drunkard; (7) the prison brigade; (8) the poor man's bank; (9) the poor man's lawyer; (10) Whitechapel-by-the-sea.

Nearly all of the scheme that Booth conceived is found in the work of the Army today.

CLOSING YEARS OF THE GENERAL'S LIFE

During the closing years of his life, the General spent much of his time visiting, impressing, and advising his followers in every country of the globe. Preaching was again his chief objective, and he left much of his social reform program to the hands of others. Old age crept upon him, but his will was unbroken and his spirit undaunted. In 1902, King Edward VI invited the General officially to be present at the coronation. When visiting in foreign countries, he was received by important political and business people everywhere. A suburban villa in North London was his final permanent home. But his restless, active spirit would not allow him to retire to the quiet and peace of his home. Each year it drove him all about the earth, until his failing eyesight forced him to give up his travels. The General was to spend his last days in total blindness. By August, 1912, William Booth had lost his strength and much of his memory. The last few days of his life were spent without speaking. On the evening of August 20, 1912, during a storm, the General quietly passed away with eighty-three active years behind him, leaving a movement that is indeed his monument.

LASTING ACCOMPLISHMENTS AND PERMANENT SIGNIFICANCE

General Booth placed life above theological differences. He believed in social reform, but religion was the core of his program. He is a shining example to the physically handicapped and to those who are mentally persecuted, for he had to face the opposition of ill health, his father's family, his friends, his church, the intellectuals of England, and even on the part of his own children. His social reforms, in all probability, will not live forever, but they have contributed much to a class of people that was greatly in need of help. His passion for social justice will stand with the strength of the everlasting hills. The Salvation Army, which he founded and for whose perpetuation he made provision, is today world wide and is exerting a powerful influence where the church does not function. So strong is its organization and so great is its loyalty that it bids fair to last long into the future. Finally, William Booth has permanent significance because of his own personal character. He believed that civilization is great only when it is built upon the rock of the moral law. He perceived the insufficiency of the human reason and arrived at the truth that the Infinite may be clasped and held by the upstretched hands of love and faith.

One of his biographers has said: "Do we not come as close as is possible to the truth of this man when we say that had he been one of the Twelve, Simon Peter would not have been alone when he stepped out upon the Sea of Galilee?"[2]

For Discussion

1. Since the churches are becoming more and more social conscious, is there any longer any need for the Salvation Army?
2. With the coming of the Social Security Act in the United States and similar acts in other countries, is there any longer a need for the "social scheme" of General Booth?
3. Is the rigid military system of the Salvation Army consistent with the democratic spirit in modern society?
4. Does the personnel of the Salvation Army officers show any advance in the educational and cultural level over that of, let us say, a half century ago?
5. Why not plan to visit an Army station, proceeding from the open-air meeting to the Salvation Army Hall, and make full inquiry concerning the work of the Army in your city or district?

For Further Reading

Begbie, Harold. *William Booth, the Founder of the Salvation Army.* London, Macmillan, 1920.

Booth-Tucker, Frederick. *William Booth, the General of the Salvation Army.* New York, The Salvation Army Printing and Publishing Company, 1898.

Memoirs of Catherine Booth. New York, Revell, 1892.

Friederichs, Hulda. *The Romance of the Salvation Army.* London, Cassell, 1907.

Outlines of Salvation Army History. London, General Salvationist Publishing and Supply, Ltd., 1928.

[2] Begbie, Harold. *William Booth, the Founder of the Salvation Army.* London, Macmillan, 1920, Vol. II, p. 486.

Walter Rauschenbusch

by

G. Walter Fiske

Emeritus Professor of Practical Theology
Oberlin Graduate School of Theology

A man of simple life, of genuine humility, and quiet tastes, Walter Rauschenbusch would never in his life have claimed to be a prophet. Scholar, teacher, minister, preacher, theologian, historian, social worker, and great lover of the poor—he was all of these. Yet the world knows him best as *a prophet of social justice*. Though a quiet, mild-mannered person, a lover of peace, and naturally shunning publicity, his keen sense of justice and loyalty to truth and duty ultimately drove him to champion the rights of the oppressed and underprivileged as fearlessly as the ancient prophets, Amos and Isaiah, but always in the kindly spirit of Jesus Christ, the Master he uncompromisingly obeyed and adored. The key to his brave, strong, sacrificial life was simply his love for Christ and fellow men.

His birthplace and always his home city was Rochester, New York, where his father, Augustus Rauschenbusch, was also professor in Rochester Theological Seminary. Descendant of an unbroken line of seven evangelical German ministers, and his own father born in the "Vaterland," yet he was a thoroughly loyal American, as his published words declare: "I was born an American citizen, as you know, and have never dreamed of being anything else. The American ideals of democracy have dominated my intellectual life. I am not merely an American in sentiment, but have taken our democratic principles very seriously and used my life to inculcate them and spread them here and abroad." Yet the family's high regard for German education led him to take his junior college work in a classical school in Guetersloh, Germany, where he graduated with first honors. Later, he received his A.B. degree from the University of Rochester, and took his theological course there also, in his father's Seminary.

A SHEPHERD OF THE POOR

Graduating in 1886, at the age of twenty-five, he accepted the pastorate of the Second German Baptist Church in New York City. It was a parish of immigrant laboring people in a crowded tenement district, and there, with his brave young wife, he put in eleven hard years of sacrificial service as the shepherd of the poor. With utter unselfishness, denying himself all luxuries, he lived only for his people, and his devotion won their loving appreciation in a wonderful degree.

When young Rauschenbusch started his hard work in that tenement parish, he had given twenty years of his life to study; a long, patient, expensive preparation. Yet for salary, he took what his people could afford to pay, *only six hundred dollars,* and he pinched, skimped, and managed to live on it. It was about the same pittance his people were existing on. They loved him all the more for living on their level, and felt his real sympathy. Up the long flights of stairs he climbed to find them in their three- to seven-story tenements and sweatshops. Into the hospitals, saloons, police courts, and prisons he followed them in their misfortunes and their wanderings. He brought back home their prodigals. He shared their family joys, griefs, and holidays. He brightened their days with his perennial good cheer, his scintillating humor, and his boundless faith. He shared with them his wonderful vitality of body, mind, and spirit, and it fed their souls. All the while, he tried to preach the gospel to them, the gospel as it had been preached unto him, to save their souls and his. He found it helped greatly; but it did not solve the awful social problems that engulfed his people. He wearied of telling them God would be good to them in the next world. What about their rights in *this* world?

Gradually, he made the discovery that the old-fashioned "simple gospel" was not enough, and it was not the whole gospel of Christ. His poor parishioners were swamped by social injustice. Souls saved on Sunday were lost again by the following Saturday night, and no wonder. Even for the sake of spiritual conservation, some sort of *social* redemption was imperative. The community itself must be cleansed, lifted, redeemed. Souls are not really saved in a vacuum. Men must be saved in their social relations and groups, or they are not really saved at all. Unjust groups must be saved from group sin. For as he himself so clearly states it, "There are two great entities in human life, the human soul and the human race, and religion is to save both."

So back to his New Testament he went with redoubled energy on his quest for the truth as it is in Jesus; and with eyes freshly opened to a great human need, he found that Jesus agreed with him, that the real religion of Jesus is a social religion and always has been—a religion of brotherly living as well as the worship of God. According to the Nazarene Carpenter, a man is only half a Christian who merely loves God and tries to save his selfish soul. He must also love his brother men and prove it by unselfish, brotherly life.

THE GOSPEL OF THE KINGDOM

Thus, early in his pastorate, he discovered and preached the "Social Gospel." He preached it with the conviction of a great life-passion. It was simply the recovery of Jesus' own emphasis on the good news of the Kingdom of God. According to the record, the first text on which Jesus preached was "Repent ye, for the Kingdom of heaven is at hand." To young Rauschenbusch this meant the Kingdom of God's Good Will, the reign of God on earth; and the sins to be repented of were not merely their sins against God, but sins of cruel injustice to men.

Some said then, and still say now, that this is not what the coming of the Kingdom meant to Jesus. In spite of Jesus' own definition of the Kingdom in the Lord's prayer: "Thy Kingdom come: [i.e.] thy will be done on earth as in heaven," some scholars claim he accepted wholly the nearsighted view of the popular eschatology of his day. They say that all Jesus had in mind was the apocalyptic hope of the radical Jewish nationalists who fondly expected the sudden coming of the New Age—Jehovah's miraculous intervention to drive out their powerful enemies and restore the kingdom of David in the Holy City. To be sure, this would be terribly belittling Jesus, not merely as a petty nationalist, but also making him out as woefully mistaken. Rauschenbusch could not do that. He was too good a biblical scholar either to overlook the eschatological passages in the words of Jesus or to make them central in his teachings.

What if Jesus did expect a great crisis, a sudden upheaval and a New Age within a very few years? Our friend could not conceive of Jesus' preaching so magnificent a gospel of good will as mere "interim ethics." If it was right for two years, it was everlastingly just and right. If the golden rule and the law of love furnished the only foundation for right human relations in the few years before the coming Jewish crisis in the first century, the same foundation must be eternally right and essential for the building of a brotherly world in all the centuries to come. The Kingdom of God can mean nothing but the Reign of God, the kind of a world in which God's good will is supreme and men learn to live in peace and brotherhood. So, with an enthusiasm born of his loyalty to Christ and his devotion to his needy people, whose lives were so pitifully meager and unjustly thwarted, he challenged his generation to build a spiritual commonwealth of God, a gradual heaven on earth. He declared that the Kingdom of God must be the transformation of the social order into a kingdom of righteousness. Well he knew the dangers of this doctrine. There was social dynamite in it. He would inevitably make enemies; but this never deterred him; his brave soul never flinched. Wherever conscience led, he followed the path of duty, living the gospel that he preached, preaching without reservations the whole gospel he believed, studying laboriously to know the will of God and the mind of Christ that he might believe only the truth, and putting his whole strength into the task of shepherding his people for eleven faithful years.

A CALL TO LEADERSHIP

It is easy to see the providence of God calling Walter Rauschenbusch back to Rochester. His arduous years in New York as a parish minister had seasoned his character and produced a beautiful spirit. A year of graduate study abroad, meanwhile, had helped to make him a biblical and theological specialist, and his persistent study of the Gospels further prepared him to teach the New Testament at Rochester in his own father's footsteps. Then, after five years, he became professor of church history.

Throughout his teaching career of twenty-one years, he was

handicapped by an affliction that would have kept most men out of the teaching profession. The fact that he was almost completely deaf before leaving New York makes his call to Rochester a remarkable recognition of high character and unusual ability. It was the fine quality of the man that they wanted, his sweet spirit, his religion of sacrificial devotion, fully as much as his expert wisdom. And though his deafness was a great privation, cutting him off from the beautiful world of sound and music, the affliction was borne with an amazing patience worthy of a St. Francis. It was in itself a badge of sainthood, for it was the price he paid for his unmitigated faithfulness to duty. It reminded his friends of the Good Shepherd who scaled the icy heights in quest of his one hundredth sheep that was lost, and the cost of his devotion ere he found it and laid it on his shoulders rejoicing. For our Shepherd of the Tenements, suddenly called out on an errand of mercy in mid-winter, left his sick-bed in a severe illness and ventured out in a bitter winter storm. The premature exposure cost him his hearing, but with joy unabated he went on with his sacrificial service. His was a soldierly spirit. Perfect obedience to the will of God was the rule of his life. In spite of his deafness, he went on to Rochester, taught for twenty-one years with an assistant at his elbow with pencil and a pad of paper, and made that teacher's desk a radiating center of spiritual energy and amazing outreach into the world.

HIS EXPANDING INFLUENCE THROUGH BOOKS

As with most prophets, though his challenging voice reached many thousands, his printed words have aroused and stimulated millions. When he died, Dr. Steiner, of Grinnell, testified, "His loss to the church and to the Kingdom of God is so great as to be immeasurable now; but as with all the prophets, he will live and speak and continue to speak as long as his message will be needed." And President Faunce, of Brown University, added: "I do not know of any Christian writer in this country who has more largely influenced the thinking of his fellow men." This remarkable influence came from his six outstanding books: *Christianity and the Social Crisis* (1907); *Prayers of the Social Awakening* (1910); *Christianizing the Social Order* (1912); *Dare We Be Christians?* (1914);

Social Principles of Jesus (1916); and *A Theology For the Social Gospel* (1917).

Few books have been written with more definite purpose and consecrated passion. Doctor Rauschenbusch lectured in his classroom on church history, but his life enthusiasm was the Kingdom of God, his life passion was to help bring in that reign of God's good will in a redeemed humanity. The product, of course, of his decade of ministry to the needy in his New York parish, all six books are aflame with a holy indignation that in a nominally Christian country there was still so much injustice and lack of pity. His books challenged the church to teach and live the whole gospel of Jesus. They aroused a dormant, complacent church. Thousands of ministers caught fire from his flaming messages. After a re-study of the New Testament, they proclaimed in a thousand pulpits the social message of the Man of Galilee with which the Rauschenbusch books had thrilled them. To be sure, Jesus had promoted no social program. He had laid down no rules save the Golden Rule of kindness. Yet he had clearly taught the preciousness of a single human life, the nobility of manual labor, the dignity of the personal rights of women and children, the perennial need of childlikeness, the power of kindness even to conquer enemies, the greatness of humility, of forgiveness, of true neighborliness that knows no limits, the greatness of unselfish service, the glory of sacrificial love, and the duty of the strong to help the weak and allow none to exploit them. Clearly Jesus cared less for ritual worship than for justice and righteous living. His religion is *love in action,* a far more costly thing than a cheap religion of easy beliefs, creeds, and sacraments.

The flaming challenge of the Rauschenbusch books lies in his courageous testing of our modern social order by these principles of Jesus. Most churches and ministers had not dared to do this. Our Rochester prophet dared to make a moral diagnosis of our politics, our business, our social living, just as Jesus showed up the cruel injustice and pious hypocrisy of his day. As bravely as Amos of old, he dared to write: "Insofar as rich men have been mere accumulators of unearned wealth, they need expect no praise from the future. There is nothing in ethics, in politics, or in economics that makes the swollen fortunes of our day desirable or admirable. Our system of private ownership has disconnected the power of the strong from the service of the community and has concentrated it on the accumulation of private wealth."[1] Elsewhere he defends the sacred right of private ownership and demands its wider extension; but he insists that if our social order is to be Christianized, the increase of wealth by unjust means must cease. Only when profit is the fair return for useful service is it on a Christian basis. Any other kind of profit makes chasms between classes, increases poverty, and arouses bitter hatred. Our friend was no more hostile to the rich than Jesus was, but with Jesus' own sympathy he championed the cause of the poor, and his books are full of concrete facts and a vast deal of sociological research proving the social and economic injustice of the times.

SOME CAUSES HE ADVOCATED

In general, Dr. Rauschenbusch conceived of the ideal Christian community and state as a co-operative commonwealth. He insisted that the rights of all persons and all classes must be safeguarded, including co-operation among both employers and employees, and the fundamental right of collective bargaining. The general welfare requires a higher standard of living for the laboring classes. This includes an increased share in profits, a shorter working day, better housing and working conditions to conserve physical fitness and working efficiency, and protection from occupational hazards and diseases. These are the fundamental concern of a Christian civilization. He urged technical education for every worker, a connectional system of employment bureaus, and elimination of slums, grafting politicians, and all extortionate leadership in both politics and business. "The type of business leadership which took millions out of filthy factory towns, wore out women and took their youth from children, cleared twelve per cent from slum tenements, kept men and women by high prices and fear of the future—this type of leadership is antiquated." This is the appeal he "made hopefully to the educated reason and the moral insight of modern Christian men" in his *Social Principles of Jesus.*[2]

He insists that social Christianity is creating a new type of man

[1] Rauschenbusch, Walter. *Christianizing the Social Order.* New York, Macmillan, p. 305.

[2] New York, Association Press, 1916, p. 109.

that respects human personality in every individual irrespective of race, sex, sect, or color. Christian democracy must guarantee fraternity of all races and nations and social classes. Even the criminal must be treated fairly, and all defectives, delinquents, and underprivileged, in the spirit of Christ, though the destructive forces of society must be restrained to safeguard the rights of all persons. War he hated with a holy hatred, wearing black crêpe upon his sleeve from 1914 to his death in July, 1918. War is caused by the lust for unearned, unjust gain, and must be relegated to the barbarism from whence it came. Small nations must be rescued from the imperialistic tyranny of the powerful; and all nations must be saved from their own cruel militarism. This problem of international peace and disarmament is the problem of expanding Christian love and brotherhood. God wills it. It will come with his victorious Kingdom of Good Will.

A LIFE OF DEEP PERSONAL PIETY

All this profound emphasis on the social religion of Jesus, and its application to our human needs today, was the genuine religion of Walter Rauschenbusch. But none who knew him ever doubted that his religion was fed from the invisible springs of prayer and constant communion with God. This is revealed in this poetic gem, one of his later writings:

THE LITTLE GATE TO GOD

In the castle of my soul
Is a little postern gate,
Whereat, when I enter,
I am in the presence of God.
In a moment, in the turning of a thought,
I am where God is.
This is a fact.

The world of men is made of jangling noises.
With God is a great Silence,
But that Silence is a melody
Sweet as the contentment of love,
Thrilling as a touch of flame.

When I enter into God,
All life has a meaning,
Without asking I know;
My desires are even now fulfilled,
My fever is gone
In the great quiet of God.
My troubles are but pebbles on the road,
My joys are like the everlasting hills.

So it is when my soul steps through the postern gate
Into the presence of God.
Big things become small, and small things become great.
The near becomes far, and the future is near.
The lowly and despised is shot through with glory.
God is the substance of all revolutions;
When I am in Him, I am in the Kingdom of God
And in the Fatherland of my Soul.

No wonder that of such a Christian it could be said, "No man since the Church began has done more to set Christendom praying on social problems." And gratefully his friend, Rev. John Howard Melish, asks, "Where in the entire anthology of Christian prayer can be found a prayer like this of his?"[3]

A PRAYER FOR HEAVEN ON EARTH

O God we praise thee for the dream of the golden city of peace and righteousness which has ever haunted the prophets of humanity, and we rejoice with joy unspeakable that at last the people have conquered the freedom and knowledge and power which may avail to turn into reality the vision that so long has beckoned in vain.

Speed now the day when the plains and the hills and the wealth thereof shall be the people's own, and thy freemen shall not live as tenants of men on the earth which thou hast given to all; when no babe shall be born without its equal birthright in the riches and knowledge wrought out by the labor of the ages; and when the mighty engines of industry shall throb with a gladder music because the men who ply their great tools shall be their owners and masters.

We pray thee to revive in us the hardy spirit of our forefathers that we may establish and complete their work, building on the basis of their

[3] *Churchman*, September 14, 1918.

democracy the firm edifice of a co-operative commonwealth, in which both government and industry shall be of the people, by the people, and for the people. May we who now live see the oncoming of the great day of God, when all men shall stand side by side in equal worth and real freedom, all toiling and all reaping, masters of nature and brothers of men, exultant in the tide of the common life, and jubilant in the adoration of thee, the source of their blessings and the Father of all.

And Doctor Melish adds, "I have seen men who told me they were not religious and had no use for the Church bow their heads in that prayer, and at its close say, as the expression of something deep within them, 'AMEN.'"

For Discussion

1. What was Dr. Rauschenbusch's especially helpful training for a life of leadership in social religion?
2. How did his years of experience as a shepherd of the poor help him to understand the brotherly teachings of Jesus?
3. What special teachings of Jesus had profound influence upon his thinking, teaching, and writing?
4. What were the outstanding traits of character in this great soul that won the love and admiration of thousands of American Christians?
5. What messages in his books, for the building of a better world and the Kingdom of God, have given you a fresh vision of what Jesus' own prayer meant: "Thy Kingdom Come?"

For Further Reading

Rochester Theological Seminary Record, The Rauschenbusch Number, November, 1918.

Singer, Anna M. *Walter Rauschenbusch and His Contribution to Social Christianity.* Boston, Badger, 1926.

Baker, R. S. "Walter Rauschenbusch." *American Magazine,* December, 1909.

"Walter Rauschenbusch." *Dictionary of American Biography,* New York, Scribner, Vol. XV, 1935.

See also books by Walter Rauschenbusch.

John Calvin

by

GEORGIA HARKNESS
Professor of Applied Theology
Garrett Biblical Institute

EARLY LIFE

JOHN CALVIN was born at Noyon, a town in Picardy fifty-eight miles north of Paris, on July 10, 1509. He died in Geneva on May 27, 1564. Between these dates is compressed one of the most vigorous and influential lives in the history of the Christian Church. It is a life of many lights and shadows, of great faults and great virtues. It is a life lived powerfully, though not always serenely, for the glory of God. Calvin's close associate and first biographer, Theodore Beza, wrote of him, "As it is easy for malevolence to calumniate his character, so the most exalted virtue will find it difficult to imitate his conduct." This verdict still holds true.

Calvin was a precocious and serious-minded youth, and at the age of fourteen he entered the University of Paris. There he displayed unusual skill in Latin and argumentation, and thus laid the foundation for his ability in later life to write theology in Latin of remarkable clarity and vigor. His father had intended that he enter the priesthood of the Catholic church, but when he completed the work of the university at nineteen, the father, influenced by a church quarrel and the hope of more lucrative returns, sent him to Orleans to study law. Calvin was destined to be a theologian rather than a lawyer, but this legal training left a permanent stamp upon his thought.

Finishing his law course, Calvin went back to Paris to study the classics, and there published in 1532 his first book, a commentary on Seneca's *Treatise on Clemency*. Sometime within the next year occurred the most crucial event of his life: his conversion to Protestantism. Though Calvin wrote voluminously, we have no exact account of how this happened. He speaks of his conversion as coming direct from God. Contributing factors were doubtless his contact with certain Protestant friends, study of the New Testament, and the general ferment that was pervading Europe as a result of the preaching of Luther and Zwingli. Though the causes are obscure, the results are clear. From that time on, he was to give up a life of scholarly quiet to court poverty and conflict in obedience to what he believed to be the will of God.

Because of suspicion connected with the expression of Protestant sentiments by his friend Nicholas Cop, rector of the University, Calvin was forced to flee from Paris. After some months of retirement, he came to Basel. There in March, 1536, he published the first edition of one of the most important theological treatises ever written, his *Institutes of the Christian Religion*. This went through five editions in his lifetime, and was greatly expanded but not essentially changed. The doctrines expressed in it that are most characteristic of Calvin's thought are the absolute sovereignty of God, man's sinfulness and helplessness apart from God, and the predestination by God of the "elect" to whom he offers salvation. These doctrines did not originate with Calvin, being found in the thought of Paul, Augustine, and Luther, but through his *Institutes* he did much to promulgate them. The book is the most logical and readable exposition of Protestant doctrine that the age of the Reformation produced, and its first draft shows amazing maturity for a youth of twenty-six.

By one of those minor incidents which sometimes alter the course of history, Calvin's life work was destined to be located in Geneva. Traveling to Noyon to settle his father's estate, he planned upon his return to go to Strassburg. But, finding the regular route blocked by war, he went by way of Geneva and stopped to spend the night. There he found the Protestant pastor, William Farel, overwhelmed with more than he could handle in the management of this gay, liberty-loving, newly Protestant city. Farel laid upon Calvin's conscience that it was his duty to come to Geneva as one of its ministers. Though Calvin was reluctant to give up the quiet life of study that awaited him at Strassburg, he heard in Farel's words the call of the

Lord. He yielded, and in August, 1536, there began an epoch-making pastorate.

THE THEOCRACY IN GENEVA

The term theocracy, "rule of God," means the rule of those regarded as God's representatives, the officials of the Church. So thoroughly has this become associated with the Geneva of Calvin's day that it is difficult to realize that its establishment presented any difficulties. However, Calvin had to fight for power through many more years than he was able to enjoy the fruits of victory.

To understand what happened, it is necessary to understand something of Calvin's theory of the relations of the Church and the State, and also something of his temperament. There was as yet no clearly defined principle of the separateness of Church and State such as we have in America, nor was there a state church like the Church of England today. For centuries there had been quarrels, settled by rough compromises, between emperors and Popes, and the rise of Protestantism now brought the issue again sharply into the foreground. Calvin conceived of Church and State as two distinct institutions, each with its own jurisdiction and functions. Yet he placed the Church above the State, and held that in case of clash its authority should be supreme because it represented the word and will of God. Any affront to the Church was an affront to God. Similarly, he regarded himself and the other ministers at Geneva as God's representatives, and this meant that to oppose the ministers was to oppose God.

How large a part his personal desire for power played in the struggle it is difficult to say, for personal ambition and religious loyalty often have a curious way of becoming intermingled. Yet if one reads the story without prejudice, it is clear, even in its most gruesome pages, that Calvin sincerely thought he was doing the will of God. When he was convinced that any course of action was right, he went ahead with invincible determination, unstopped by any distress it might bring upon himself or others.

As soon as Calvin became pastor at Geneva, he began vigorously to work along the lines that were to dominate his entire future policy: the establishment of *purity of doctrine* and *purity of morals*. A Confession of Faith was drawn up, to which everybody was expected to give assent. Laws were passed forbidding such practices as gambling, the singing of frivolous songs, and the possession of images. Everybody was compelled to attend the Protestant service. There were many in Geneva who objected, some because they were Catholic sympathizers, and others, the Libertines, because they were free-thinkers and free-livers who did not wish to submit to such discipline.

Civil affairs were in the hands of a Council, but it soon became evident that there was no clear line of division between civil and religious matters. Not only did the Council pass edicts regulating private morals and church attendance, but it began also, contrary to Calvin's wishes, to try to prescribe the form in which the sacraments were to be administered and to claim the right of excommunication. The issue became acute in the spring of 1538. Calvin and Farel refused to accede to the Council's wishes regarding the use of unleavened bread in the sacrament, and they were ordered to leave the city. Calvin's comment upon this decree reveals his spirit, "Well indeed! If we had served men, we should have been ill rewarded, but we serve a greater Master who will recompense us."

Driven from Geneva, Calvin journeyed to Strassburg, where he lived in poverty but in satisfying activity for the next three years. There he accepted a position as preacher and professor of theology. He revised the form of public worship, introduced congregational singing, and established the sermon-centered type of Sunday service, which has been retained to the present in most Calvinistic churches. Also, being now nearly thirty and still a bachelor, he cast about him a somewhat calculating eye and married in 1540 the wife who was to be his companion until her death in 1549. When she died, he paid her the high compliment of saying that she had never in any way interfered with his work! Calvin's was not a life of intimate companionship, but of dedication to public tasks.

Meanwhile, the church at Geneva, which had not been able to get along with him, had discovered that they could not get along without him! Deprived of his organizing hand, matters fell into such confusion that a delegate was dispatched to urge him to return. Calvin went reluctantly, knowing that trouble awaited him, but again with a sense of divine leadership. He consented, he says, in order not to be of "those who have more care for their own ease and profit than for the edification of the Church." On September 13, 1541, he quietly re-entered Geneva and resumed his ministry.

It will be impossible in this survey to carry his story through all the vicissitudes of the years from 1541 until 1555, when his control of the city became undisputed. The Libertines were ever in the offing to oppose him either by political power or by the subtler forces of ridicule. In order to make the Church independent of the State in spiritual matters, he drew up an ecclesiastical constitution, called the *Ordonnances,* and succeeded in having it adopted with some modification. Its purpose was not only to define more precisely the relations of the church officials to civil rulers but to establish a new ecclesiastical body, the Consistory, to represent the Church in its guardianship of faith and morals. The result was repeated clashes between the Consistory and the Council, particularly over power of excommunication, which was not finally lodged in the Consistory's jurisdiction until 1555.

The main tasks of the Consistory were to compel church attendance and police the morals of the church members. It could admonish and give public censure, but overt punishment had to be meted out by the Council. Some of the offenses for which the Consistory admonished and the Council punished would not in our day seem very reprehensible! The records show that penalties were meted out, without respect of persons, for dancing, playing cards on Sunday, spending time in taverns, betrothing one's daughter to a Catholic, having one's fortune told by gypsies, eating fish on Good Friday, shaving the tonsure on a priest's head, saying there is no devil or hell, criticizing the doctrine of election, calling the Pope a good man, singing a song defamatory to Calvin. Other offenses of a more serious nature, such as theft or adultery, naturally received condemnation and stringent punishment.

Calvin took seriously his mission to clean up the morals of the city. One incident may illustrate his thoroughness. The taverns were sinks of iniquity. Accordingly, he had them closed and "abbayes" substituted. These were to be under the charge of respectable persons, and bread and wine were to be sold at cost. No swearing or slandering was to be permitted, no dancing or indecency, no singing of obscene songs. Religious conversation was encouraged;

one must say grace over his food and drink before partaking, and return thanks afterward. Then, at nine o'clock one was to go home in a sober and godly frame of mind! This "noble experiment" was short lived, but Geneva was a cleaner city for having tried it. In fact, whatever may be thought of his methods, Calvin wrought so effectively for cleaner morals in Geneva that the city was called by John Knox "the most perfect school of Christ that ever was on earth since the days of the apostles."

PERSECUTION OF HERETICS

Other matters of more serious consequence were the actions taken against heretics. It is these which most stain Calvin's memory, for although restrictions in private morals were often irksome, the penalties imposed were not serious. Calvin's attitude toward heresy caused the high-minded Sebastian Castellio to be excluded from the Genevan ministry for questioning the inspiration of the Song of Solomon. It caused Jacques Gruet to be beheaded for belittling the Mosaic Law and writing "All nonsense" in one of Calvin's books arguing for the immortality of the soul. It caused the Spanish physician Michael Servetus to be burned at the stake for holding what would now be regarded as a rather mild form of Unitarianism. The events connected with Servetus' execution are very complicated, but even the most favorable interpretation cannot absolve Calvin from responsibility.

It is, however, important to see *why* Calvin persecuted heretics. And this is difficult for one to understand whose thinking is saturated with the idea of religious freedom. In part, Calvin was the child of his age, and to behead or burn another for difference of opinion was not so uncommon then as now. In part, also, he did it out of protecting care for those whom he profoundly believed were being injured—not in body, but worse yet, in *soul*—by the poison of false doctrines. When wolves are about to devour the sheep, it is the kindest policy—so such reasoning runs—to kill the wolves and save the sheep. Furthermore, he believed that heresy dishonored God. At any needful cost to men, God's honor must be upheld.

In many matters Calvin's standards were not those of our day. There is no clearer evidence of progress than the fact that we so spontaneously condemn him for consenting to the death of a person whose most serious offense was to differ in theology. But before we condemn Calvin, we should earn the right to do so by approximating his religious devotion and sincerity. His errors were those of judgment as to what *is* the will of God, never of moral flabbiness in doing it.

DECLINING YEARS

From 1555 until his death in 1564, Calvin was master of Geneva. One is tempted to call him dictator, but dictators do not labor so selflessly as he for the glory of God. In 1559 the Council honored him by conferring upon him citizenship. He had now lived in Geneva for twenty years. No native son could have served its interests more zealously, but he seems never to have sought to become a citizen. He was as little attracted by pecuniary as by civic rewards. He asked for little and lived simply, and he gave generously to those in need. When he died he left a spiritual inheritance of unestimated value and a material estate of between fifteen hundred and two thousand dollars. These facts ought to be noted, not in overglorification of his character, but in reply to the charges of autocracy and self-seeking often flung at him. It meant much to him that his office as minister of the Church of God should be respected, and he was willing to fight for its recognition with stern intensity. Yet he did not look upon himself as other than a servant of God who had been called to the leadership of the Genevan church.

In 1559, two further events of much importance took place. One was the publication of the fifth and last edition of the *Institutes*. The other was the establishment of the University of Geneva, which has ever since occupied an important place in European—and in fact, in international—education. There had long been a school at Geneva, provision for free compulsory education having been made by Farel before Calvin arrived. However, in order to provide better facilities both for general and religious education, Calvin in 1558 induced the Council to erect more buildings, enlarge the faculty, and raise the school to collegiate rank. Theodore Beza, who was later to be Calvin's successor in the pastorate, was installed as rector, and the university was soon attracting students from all over western Europe. Although Calvin's primary motive was probably to provide adequate training for the ministry, he had also a profound sense of the importance of an educated laity.

Calvin's declining years were full of herculean labors—preaching, lecturing, writing, strengthening the various Reformed churches, ministering to the needs of persons in his parish. A fragment that suggests the pressure of such activities reads:

> When the messenger called for my book, I had twenty sheets to revise (I had) to preach, to read to the congregation, to write four letters, to attend some controversies, and to return answers to more than ten persons who interrupted me in the midst of my labors for advice.

Calvin worked with indefatigable industry, for he had the temperament of one who can drive himself for the accomplishment of a chosen end. One must work with untiring zeal when one labors for the glory of God!

Yet even a soul of triple bronze must be encased in a human body. From his student days Calvin had been subject to severe attacks of indigestion, which were doubtless both a cause and a result of the attacks of violent anger which sometimes overcame him. By 1563 he began also to show symptoms of tuberculosis, and it was evident that he had not long to live. He continued to preach when he could not walk, and a graphic etching shows him being carried through the streets to his pulpit in a chair. When unable to preach, he still carried on an extensive correspondence from his room, and gave counsel to many. He must work while God gave him strength.

On May 27, 1564, Calvin died. The next day he was buried like any humble citizen, without pomp or ceremony. It was his wish that his burial be modest and that no monument should mark his restingplace. In the cemetery of Plain-palais the visitor is shown a slab of stone that bears the initials J. C., but "no man knoweth of his sepulchre unto this day."

Calvin was only fifty-five when he died. But to few men is it given to round out so fully the work of a life. Purity of faith and purity of living, as he envisaged these, had become the dominant temper of Geneva. The ecclesiastical system for which he had fought was established. The *Institutes* had assumed their final form; the University was in operation. All that remained was for

Calvin's principles to take further root in Europe, and spreading to America, to become the undergirding moral foundation of a new world.

To a greater degree than most men realize, we are still the spiritual heirs of Calvin. The primary Calvinistic virtues were industry, thrift, honesty, sobriety, chastity, Sabbath observance, and a great sense of the glory of God. Largely through Puritan influence these became the primary American virtues. They are not so highly prized now as they once were. In softening the rigor of Calvinism, we lost many of its rough edges—but with them, some of the granite underneath. Is it better so? Each must judge for himself.

This life, dedicated to the glory of God, was austere—but it had about it a certain grandeur found only in lives that are centered about high ends. It is symbolized, in our day, by the austere simplicity of a New England meetinghouse with its white spire pointing heavenward. Calvin's memory, if we can forget the dark shadows and see its true foundations, seems to be saying:

> "I will extol thee, my God, O King;
> And I will bless thy name for ever and ever. . . .
> Great is the Lord, and greatly to be praised;
> And his greatness is unsearchable."[1]

For Discussion

1. What factors in Calvin's early life contributed to his subsequent work?
2. What, if anything, is wrong with Calvin's theory of the relation between church and state?
3. Would Calvin have been more effective in Geneva if he had demanded less?
4. Why is it wrong to persecute those of different theological belief? Why did Calvin think he was justified in doing so?
5. To what factors in his environment, temperament, or religious outlook do you attribute his remarkable power?

[1] Psalms 145: 1 and 3.

For Further Reading

Reyburn, Hugh Y. *John Calvin.* London, Hodder and Stoughton, 1914.

Walker, Williston. *John Calvin.* New York, Putnam, 1906.

Foster, H. D. *Collected Papers.* Privately printed, 1929.

Smith, Preserved. *The Age of the Reformation.* New York, Holt, 1920.

Harkness, Georgia. *John Calvin: The Man and His Ethics.* New York, Holt, 1931.

St. Paul

by

LOIS R. ROBISON
Author
Bronxville, N. Y.

"Hear, O Israel:
Jehovah our God is one Jehovah:
And thou shalt love Jehovah thy God
With all thy heart,
And with all thy soul,
And with all thy might."[1]

IN THE Hall of Hewn Stone, a young and valiant Cilician Jew faced the hostile Council. In the eyes of the presiding judges there was no glint of mercy. On the faces of the rabid crowd, close pressing and blood hungry, were written no messages of sympathy or understanding. The beautiful, eloquent words of the young prisoner at the bar brought no murmurs of approval, no clapping of hands. But even in this sinister picture there was a figure more bitter, more intent to show no pity, more determined that no life be spared, more unrelenting in his desire that the law which had said "but you shall surely kill him, You shall stone him with stones that he die," be fulfilled.

That prisoner was Stephen. That sternest accuser and unrelenting judge was Saul, of the city of Tarsus. What fate had placed them thus, opposite to each other at such a time and place?

In the home of a tentmaker (a most profitable trade in that city, where caravans swing through narrow streets, and palaquins brushed the garments of Arabs, and Phoenician sailors stepped ashore from

[1] Deuteronomy 6:4, 5.

their anchored ships) was a little lad "advanced in the Jews' religion . . . , being exceedingly zealous for the traditions of my fathers." He was born of the tribe of Benjamin of Israel, and son of a man belonging to the strictest Pharisee sect, who was also a proud Roman citizen. In his home city of Tarsus, the boy Saul, named for Israel's first king, learned his lessons and learned his trade. Eagerly his mind enriched itself with the great and moving stories of his people's past, and just as eagerly did he gather knowledge of the present—and of the far-flung empire of which he was a part. His own immediate future lay, he was sure, in the temple courts at Jerusalem, at the feet of the greatest teacher of them all, Gamaliel. And when the adolescent years came round, Saul left home and made the long and, to a boy, exciting journey "up to Jerusalem." Here for several years he learned what Moses had said, what the Law required, what the great Hillel had taught. But above all else he learned those rich prophecies that told Israel of the coming of the Glorious One, the Prince, the Son of David, the Messiah! And the day and hour of his coming? While no man knew, yet, properly interpreted, it might seem that now the time was ripe, and overripe, for the fulfillment. Where was the conquering Messiah who would lead his people and make of them an invincible kingdom? Why did he delay?

And certainly Saul was not aware that he was already here laboring and living and loving in the little northern village of Nazareth near enough so that these very students, who so longed for his coming, might have come upon him at the close of but a three days' journey.

Saul wore upon his forehead the parchment that carried the words we have printed at the head of our chapter. And he felt that he obeyed these instructions. Above all else, he thought, he "loved the Lord" and "with all his heart, and all his soul and all his might." Saul never did things by halves!

Time passed, and the youth of Nazareth had, for three years, taught that "God was love" and that "God was Spirit" and that those who worshiped him should do so "in spirit and in truth." And that he was the Son of God come "not to be ministered unto, but to minister." And had died, hanging midway between earth and sky, the shameful death of the tree, that death of which the Law taught that a man having died it must ever be accursed.

And Saul and Stephen faced each other. Stephen who said that the Messiah they awaited had already come. The earnest Stephen, unafraid, who had called his judges "stiff-necked men"—"betrayers" and "murderers." The glorified Stephen who cried, "I see the heavens opened, and the Son of man standing on the right hand of God." The beautiful Stephen who, when Saul, courageous in his stiff-necked righteous reading of the Law, and the mob had taken him to the city's outskirts and stoned him with the great, gray, jagged rocks of that place, had said, "Lord Jesus, receive my spirit." And so, smiling, had fallen asleep.

Stiffened in his unrelenting hatred of the blaspheming Nazarenes who said that the dead Jesus was risen, and haunted by the radiant martyrdom of Stephen (for Saul, courageous himself recognized unearthly courage in another when he saw it)—Saul the graduate Pharisee, Saul the young rabbi, hurried northward to root out the blasphemers, even as far north as the City of Damascus. They must be exterminated, once for all. They must be shown no mercy. He, Saul, would drag them all in chains back to Jerusalem, there to meet an ignominious death. Those dogs of Nazarenes must perish and their hateful teachings with them.

The city's gates were just ahead. But between them and the hater of the Jesus-followers there was a blinding light. From that radiance came a Voice that said, "Saul, Saul why persecutest thou me?" And in answer to Saul's awed and reverent "Who art thou, Lord?" the answer came, "I am Jesus, whom thou persecutest." No hesitation marked Saul's next words. They came at once and showed the swift acquiescence of the man, the eager need to "act."

"What wilt thou have me to do?"

No longer Saul, but now Paul, blind of eye but seeing of spirit, entered Damascus. There he begged baptism of the very group intent upon whose death he had made the journey. From there, after a period of rest and quiet and soul-searching, with physical sight restored, he started upon his many journeyings. He knew that he must prove his conversion. He knew that just acceptance was not enough for him. Paul, the Christian, could not be divorced so easily, in other people's minds, from Saul, the Nazarene-killer.

He had to earn his title to fellowship in this band, and at the same time convince his former colleagues that he was in deadly earnest, in truth a "changed man." Above all, he felt that Jesus had particularly chosen him to go out to all nations, preaching "Christ and him crucified." From the earliest days of his conversion his feet itched with the desire to take the "good news" farther and farther afield, and his tongue ached to tell the "wondrous story" to those who had never heard. Paul, the Christian, became, almost at once, Paul, the Missionary. At first he reached out to those synagogues that were within reach of Damascus. It took him only three years to prove himself and his message so dangerous to orthodox Jewry that his life was sought.

At Jerusalem, whence he fled, he received no more than a lukewarm welcome. His conversion was suspect. But it was there that he had the vision of himself sent to the Gentiles. To Caesarea and on to his homeland he went, probably spending most of his time and energy in and about his home city, Tarsus.

Several years later he became the co-worker of Barnabas, who had been sent north as a representative of the Jerusalem congregation. It was a most excellent combination. Barnabas was devotion itself, but he was also wise and gracious and quiet spoken. Paul supplied the fire and the oratory. Together they visited and preached in Cyprus, Pamphylia, Pisidia and Lycaonia. They started new congregations for the Gentiles. Always Antioch, where the Christians backed the two missionaries, was their home base. To Antioch they reported the results of their efforts and the tales of their persecutions.

At this time occurred the factional dispute that threatened to nullify all Paul's splendid work. One wing of the young Christian Church was taking a violent stand on the principle that all converts to Christianity must first signify their conversion to Judaism by circumcision. Paul, and the Church at Antioch, stood just as firmly on their contention that no such change was necessary, that all that mattered—all that anyone dared say could matter—was whether or no the convert was a "new man in Christ Jesus." And Paul and his faction won. Perhaps because of that momentous decision, you and I are Christians today, for had the narrow interpretation won, Christianity might well have become just another sect within the framework of Judaism, ingrown and flabby instead of vital, strong, and out-reaching.

But even with the decision made, not all was harmony. The *Law,* as they had always known it, still exercised great power over the more conservative leaders. Over this, or over Paul's feeling that John Mark, nephew of Barnabas, had lacked the "stuff" of which missionary Christians must be made, the two battle-scarred Christian warriors parted company, never so far as we know, to meet again.

Another phase of Paul's life was ended. But a new door, or rather many doors, opened. With young Timothy he made a tour of inspection and satisfied himself that the young churches of Galacia were growing and strong. Then he turned toward Europe, going first to Philippi. Christianity had come to Europe and into the western world through the person of Paul, the Missionary Adventurer.

Always events followed a pattern. He preached in local Jewish synagogues. He was welcomed lukewarmly by the Jews, more heartily by the Gentiles. Then his integrity was attacked by the Jews and the narrower Christian sects. They saw him as a renegade from Judaism. Fearless for himself, but anxious not to stir up any additional bitterness, Paul usually withdrew in order to still the uproar before any definite split occurred.

Athens, Corinth, and Ephesus were scenes of his labors. He grew acquainted with prison. He reaffirmed his Roman citizenship. He made a new and particularly bitter set of enemies in the Gnostics, so called because they laid claim to a special knowledge and foreknowledge of divine secrets.

In sure knowledge of his danger, he returned to Jerusalem, carrying gifts of his churches to the mother church at Jerusalem. He reported on his new stewardship to James, Jesus' own brother and recognized leader of all Christians in Jerusalem. But the Jews rose in uncontrollable rage against this man who had once been a "Pharisee of the Pharisees." They planned his death, and only the speedy arrival of the Roman garrison saved his life. In a memorable speech to the mob that was thirsting for his blood, he gave the world not only his own autobiography but his own defense as a

Jew, together with the great principles upon which he built his life as a Christian.

Then followed ten years in custody in Caesarea. Again and again the Jews tried to prove charges traitorous enough to bring about his death. Paul himself finally stood on his right of appeal to his emperor. To Rome, as a prisoner, he went.

The story of his last journey is lost to us, historically, but preserved in the traditions of the Church. Grown old in the service of the Master whom he had met on the road to Damascus, he still busied himself at work with the Christians in Rome. The Church has always held that he finally met his death by the sword in the early days of Nero's reign, when to be avowedly a Christian was to sign one's own death warrant.

Paul, a Jew of Tarsus, a Pharisee of Jerusalem, a citizen of Rome, a convert to Christ, a missionary to the Gentiles, lost his life in the capital of the world's greatest empire but found it again, we know, in "Him who strengtheneth me." Paul, more than conqueror!

Thrice was I beaten with
[Roman] rods,
Once was I stoned,
Thrice I suffered shipwreck,
A night and a day have I
been in the deep;
In journeyings often,
In perils of rivers, in perils
of robbers,
In perils from my race, in perils
from the Gentiles,
In perils in the city, in perils
in the wilderness,
In perils in the sea, in perils
among false brethren;
In labor and travail, in
watchings often,
In hunger and thirst, in
fastings often,
In cold and nakedness.[2]

---

[2] II Corinthians 11: 25-27.

For Discussion

1. List the factors that help to explain Paul's greatness.
2. Describe several of the most dramatic scenes in Paul's life.
3. What is the importance of Paul's writings?
4. Describe the strength and weakness of Paul's personality.
5. What do you consider to be Paul's outstanding contribution?

For Further Reading

Glover, T. R. *Paul of Tarsus.* New York, Harper, 1930.

Mathews, Basil. *Paul the Dauntless.* New York, Revell, 1916.

Minear, P. S. *An Introduction to Paul.* New York, Abingdon-Cokesbury, 1937.

Morton, H. V. *In the Footsteps of St. Paul.* New York, Dodd, Mead, 1936.

Wood, C. T. *Life, Letters and Religion of St. Paul.* New York, Scribner, 1925.

Nicolaus Ludwig von Zinzendorf

by

HENRY H. MEYER[1]
Professor of Religious Education
School of Theology, Boston University

NICOLAUS LUDWIG VON ZINZENDORF (Count of Zinzendorf and Pottendorf) is known to students of history as a religious and social reformer, the contemporary and close friend of Isaac Watts and John Wesley, and the honored primate (Ordinarius) and reorganizer of the Moravian Church (Unitas Fratrum). A descendant of noble ancestry, he was born at Dresden, May 26, 1700, and died on his ancestral estate at Herrnhut, near Dresden, March 19, 1760. Both of his parents belonged to the inner circle of Pietists under the personal leadership of Philip Jakob Spener, the godfather of the boy. Zinzendorf's school days were spent at Halle, the academic and missionary center of Pietism, where for a time he lived in the home of August Hermann Francke. At sixteen he went to the University of Wittenberg, where he studied law in preparation for a diplomatic career. After completing his university studies, he traveled extensively in Holland and France and throughout Germany. Having been appointed State Attorney at the Court of Saxony at the age of 21, he surrendered this important office and his contemplated diplomatic career to identify himself with a colony of Moravian refugees whom he had given shelter on his country estate at Berthelsdorf. The corner of the estate assigned to the refugees was designated Herrnhut, and here, under the leadership of Zinzendorf and a group of his close and influential friends, was established the reorganized Unity of the Brethren, perpetuated in the world-wide Moravian

[1] Grateful acknowledgment is due to the publishers for permission to quote from my book, *Child Nature and Nurture*, New York, Abingdon-Cokesbury, 1928.—H. H. M.

Church of today. For more than thirty years, 1727-1760, he inspired and in large measure personally directed and financed the effective foreign and home missionary program that has been the glory of Moravianism for more than two centuries.

During his lifetime, Zinzendorf was the central figure of the Moravian fellowship. To its guidance and work he gave all his strength and time and the major part of an independent fortune. For this fellowship he suffered exile from his native Saxony under suspicion of aiding and abetting a separatist movement in religion with heretical tendencies in theology and communistic practices in congregational organization and life. He proved himself an incessant traveler, preacher, and writer, who with singleness of purpose devoted himself to the spread and firm establishment of the new Unity of the Brethren and its unique fellowship of the Christian life.

But Zinzendorf's genius for organization was overshadowed and to a degree obscured by his passion for church unity. Like John Wesley, after the early success of the Methodist revival, Zinzendorf declined to sponsor or even encourage a separatist movement on the part of the Moravian congregations. Throughout his lifetime, the German Moravian congregations were recognized congregational units in the established Lutheran and Reformed churches, the congregation at Herrnhut being a Lutheran church in good standing. For Zinzendorf, every temporal organization of the Christian fellowship and every formal statement of creed was a concession to human need, important only as it served the spiritual purposes of that fellowship and contributed to its enrichment and wider extension. To the ideal of church unity he committed the Moravian churches to such an extent that their effective evangelistic and missionary service to the world has never during the course of two centuries degenerated into a proselyting propaganda for the extension of organized Moravianism. His brief sojourn in the American colonies, 1741-1742, principally in Pennsylvania, New York, and New Jersey, was devoted to the double purpose of evangelizing the Indians and, working among the German colonists, of bringing together into one organized fellowship, if possible, the various Protestant evangelical communions.

In the history of theology Zinzendorf appears as a Christian mystic who finds in personal Christian experience—that is, in the conscious relationship of the believer to Christ, and in the resulting life of fellowship and communion—the sum and substance of religion. Christ is himself the sum and substance of that which Zinzendorf would teach. Thus, his first book, a catechism for children, he designated *The Pure Milk of the Teachings Concerning Jesus Christ.* Throughout all his writings, from his first primer written at the age of twenty-two to his last recorded sermons and addresses the year before his death, he repeats and emphasizes over and over again the central thesis of his philosophy of salvation, the reconciliation of mankind with God through the death of Christ and the requirement that the individual should experience this reconciliation by means of a living and immediate personal faith in Christ.

While still a student at Halle, at the age of fifteen, Zinzendorf organized among his fellow students "The Order of the Mustard Seed," the members of which pledged themselves to carry or send the gospel to the neglected and the needy in the uttermost parts of the world. This vision of service Zinzendorf never lost, and in 1732 redeemed his pledge by inspiring and financing the first missionary enterprise of the reorganized Moravian Church. Under the continued encouragement of Zinzendorf and his fellow members of the Order of the Mustard Seed, the missionary work of the Moravian Brotherhood became one of the outstanding features of its work. That missionary interest and effort has never waned. In harmony with Zinzendorf's original purpose, the service of Moravian missions has been to a great extent among primitive races and in out-of-the-way places. The proportion of missionaries to church membership is about one missionary to sixty members—by far the largest in Protestantism.

His insight into child life and his understanding of the fact, if not of the laws, of spiritual growth, together with his resulting theory and practice in religious education, are among the most remarkable factors of his busy and useful life. They seem the more remarkable when it is recalled that his work belongs to an age untouched either by the scientific theory of evolution or by the modern interest in child study. Zinzendorf lived a whole century before Darwin. He preached his last sermon nearly fifty years before Herbart began to lecture on psychology at Koenigsberg. He was an older contemporary of Rousseau, but did not live to see the publication of *Emile*. He died in 1760, twenty-five years before the birth of Froebel, when Pestalozzi was still a boy of fifteen.

Three strains of religious heritage, those from Luther, Comenius, and Francke, converged in him. But to these were added native factors that made his theory and method peculiarly his own. He reflects the spirit of rebellion against the stilted artificiality of this time, which spirit likewise finds expression in Basedow and the Philanthropists, as it does in the writings of Rousseau. In the case of Zinzendorf, this rebellion was directed also against the current dogmatic catechetical teaching method of orthodox Lutheranism, and against the harsher methods of religious discipline characteristic of his time. Zinzendorf's innovations in conjunction with the refugee colony at Herrnhut led to a break with the Pietistic leaders at Halle. Because of this fact, Zinzendorf's creative work in religious pedagogy was carried on a little apart from the main line of religious-educational development, that leads directly from August Hermann Francke, through August Herman Niemeyer (the elder) to Johann Friedrich Herbart and his numerous and illustrious successors.

One outstanding impression gained from a study of the life and works of Zinzendorf, including his printed and unprinted writings and the manuscript diaries of the Pilgrim Congregation and of the congregation at Herrnhut, is that he understood and loved children, to whom he gave himself in almost daily fellowship as companion and teacher. Even when away from Herrnhut and in foreign lands, he did not give up the habit of conducting children's services and associating intimately with them. As often as possible, these days with the children were spent on some hillside meadow or in the shaded woodland. On July 9, 1755, Zinzendorf spent such a festal day with the boys and young men from Herrnhut and neighboring congregations. The report of this day, reproduced in full elsewhere, is from the Diary of the Pilgrim Congregation. After early devotions with the boys in their dormitory, Zinzendorf accompanied them on a morning walk, during which he discussed with them in an intimate, informal way their personal experiences and problems. Later, between fifty and sixty of the boys and young men continued this discussion in Zinzendorf's study. Then followed a meeting of the organized young men's group, with the consecration and admission of twenty-eight boys from the next younger group. A love feast, with an address by Zinzendorf and the partaking of the cup of covenanting by all present, brought the festivities to a close. In 1760, the year of Zinzendorf's death, we find him still conducting services with and for the children at Herrnhut as diligently as his failing health permitted, addressing them as usual at the Sunday and weekday services on January 3 and 14, March 13, 14, and 30. On April 22 he conducted the children's liturgical service. He died less than three weeks later, and at his funeral services children in large numbers took an important part.

Among the products of this association with children, extending as it did over more than thirty years, were Zinzendorf's writings for children, talks to children, and exhortations to adults about children. To the preservation of these various writings of Zinzendorf and records about him we owe such knowledge as is now available concerning his theory and practice of religious education. At the very beginning of Zinzendorf's work for the spiritual welfare of the refugee community at Herrnhut, his efforts resulted, in 1727, in an emotional revival that profoundly affected the children as well as the adults in the congregation. In commenting on this children's revival, Spangenberg mentions that the training of children was a major consideration of Zinzendorf's from the very first. The day on which the revival "broke out," August 17, has ever since been observed as a special festal day for Moravian children. In later years Zinzendorf himself looked back to this children's revival as the first clear evidence of divine approval and as the actual beginning of his lifelong work in their behalf.

Central in Zinzendorf's understanding of child nature is his recognition of the principle of free development in the individual. Free development makes for straightforwardness and self-knowledge. It prevents children from becoming hypocrites and dissemblers. The only compulsion in education normally should be that which is exerted by the teacher's example. Rules are for the most part unnecessary. Browbeaten, goody-goody children do not turn out well. Especially should arbitrary and unreasoned punishment be avoided.

Regard for the principle of free development is especially important in moral and religious training, since religion is a matter that affects the individual life as a whole, not in separate compartments. Zinzendorf endeavored to make children understand that, "Religion is the completely unified work of God in us. We think, speak, sing, and play, often feel very happy, and in all that we do, in our whole being, conduct, and everything that we undertake, we give evidence of our faith and of what is in our hearts." This principle requires that in matters of faith and conduct the younger generation shall have some freedom of choice: "We do not presume to require of a son that he should follow the same maxims as his father. In conjunction with that training which duty requires of us, we allow the greatest possible freedom." In his own household and in the bringing up of his own children, Zinzendorf put the principle of free development constantly into practice. How successfully, he asks the brethren of the congregation to judge for themselves: "My own children I have permitted to grow up and to conduct themselves without restraint and without forbidding wrongdoing except in so far as this might be harmful to society. Thus, it was possible for them to act naturally in my presence and to make of me a confidant. Whether this has succeeded, the Brethren may judge for themselves. Any other course is not permanently successful."

Thus Zinzendorf clearly recognizes the importance of safeguarding the free development of personality in the individual child. By free development he does not mean license or the elimination of social controls, but he warns against imposing restrictions or adult controls that will hamper and retard development from within. Spontaneous self-expression in free-time activities, including play, are essential to normal growth. Adult supervision of such activities should be indirect, consisting principally in setting right examples of conduct and retaining the confidence and respect of the children. This applies especially to the moral and religious development of the child. Here example is worth more than precept, and divergence from parental example in details of thought and action is to be expected of children.

Free development in the religious life and experience of the child does not mean random growth. It means growth under the inner guidance of the Holy Spirit. All human control and stimulation, such as is provided in religious and educational institutions of the community or congregation, are efforts to provide a favorable environment within which the work of the Holy Spirit in stimulating and guiding individual development will be less hampered and interfered with than in the ordinary uncontrolled environment of most children.

Zinzendorf's recognition of the principle of free development and its implications for religious experience compelled him to redefine the religious status of the child with reference to the prevailing Lutheran dogmas regarding sin and salvation. In so doing, he was never quite willing to admit—if, indeed, he himself fully recognized—the contradiction between the orthodox theological formula of baptismal regeneration and belief in the absolute moral innocence of little children. With reference to the religious status of the child, therefore, Zinzendorf the theologian is in conflict with Zinzendorf the keen observer and teacher of children. Sometimes the one and sometimes the other gains the ascendancy. Zinzendorf the theologian subscribes to the prevailing dogma regarding original sin and baptismal regeneration. Zinzendorf the pedagogue recognizes the innocence, irresponsibility, and native possibilities for good or evil of the little child. The theologian yields to the pedagogue to the extent of trying to explain away the harsher aspects of his creed and attempting a reconciliation by interpretation. The pedagogue does not yield, but insists that whatever may be the theological difficulty and need for mystical interpretation of the theological formula of salvation, the child begins life as the child of God, innocent and susceptible to both divine and human guidance, responding as naturally to the good as to the evil in its environment. What is to become of this pure, sensitive human personality-in-embryo is the problem and the responsibility of the adult community and congregation. The trust is sacred, because the life is precious and has possibilities that cannot be measured by adult experience.

Upon the occasion of his first departure for America in 1738, Zinzendorf wrote from shipboard to the congregation at Herrnhut, conveying to them what he thought might prove to be his last ecclesiastical will and testament. In this important document, "Eventual Testament," he discusses a wide range of matters affecting the life, faith, and discipline of the brotherhood. What he says concerning religious nurture and training reveals a clear recognition of the principles of religious growth paralleling physical and intellectual development. It suggests also a program for the organization of the religious community for purposes of Christian nurture. The latter is based apparently upon the actual practice already in vogue at Herrnhut and the other congregations which Zinzendorf seems to consider as still tentative and not fulfilling his ideal. His clearest and best definition of child nurture is given in this document: "What, then, is child nurture? It is a sacred, priestly method whereby souls are brought up from infancy so as not to think otherwise than that they belong to Christ and so that blessedness for them shall consist in knowing and serving him, and their greatest misfortune in becoming separated from him in any way whatsoever."

In accordance with this theory of religious growth, Zinzendorf makes provision for the nurture and cultivation of the religious life by means of grouping children and young people according to their age and religious maturity for purposes of group worship and instruction. These groups he called "choirs" in the broader sense of groups assembled for worship. In the complete organization of the religious congregation, provision was made for six separate and distinct groups, or choirs, for children and young people. These included: the "Choir of Children in Arms," a counterpart of the Cradle, or Font Roll, of the modern Sunday church school; the "Children's Choir," corresponding to the present-day primary group; choirs for boys and for girls, separate groups of junior age; choirs for older boys and for older girls; choirs for young people (sexes not separated); and choirs for various natural groupings of adults. The supervision of each choir was entrusted to elders of the congregation appointed for this purpose and known as "choir servants" or "ministers" (Chordiener). In reality, they were leaders and teachers. As the size of the group demanded, assistants or helpers were appointed. Beginning with the older boys and girls, these assistants, and in some cases the choir servants as well, were selected from the membership of the choir to which they were assigned.

The problem of religious nurture is one of preserving the child in his original innocence, keeping from him all influences that would mar or soil his spirit, and providing an environment favorable to spiritual growth. Petty rules and negative discipline are harmful. A noble example is more effective than precepts. For every age and period of spiritual development, the life experiences and example of Jesus furnish the necessary pattern. In his clear statement of these principles, Zinzendorf anticipated the conclusions of modern psychology of religion concerning original nature and the religious status and growth of the child. His statements regarding the characteristics and interests of the various age groups are brief but accurate.

In the actual work of religious education, Zinzendorf's emphasis throughout is upon the stimulation and development of religious experience rather than on the acquisition of knowledge about religion. Informal conversations about religion and group participation in religious exercises, worship, singing, Bible reading, and the exchange of personal experience are substituted for dogmatic, catechetical instruction. Religious experience is to manifest itself in attitudes and responses. Directed toward God as he has revealed himself in Christ, these attitudes and responses result in joyous intimate fellowship and conscious communion. Directed toward others and toward one's environment, they result in good will, spiritual companionship, and useful service. The religious teacher is to be the companion and trusted counselor of his pupils as well as their instructor in religion. In his emphasis upon graded instruction and training in the congregation, Zinzendorf does not overlook the importance of the home and of parental teaching. In his total plan of religious nurture and training, the place of the Christian home is central and the responsibility of parents for the religious training of their children fundamental. Therefore, parents and prospective parents, as well as children, need instruction. Where they fail in their duty, other helpers must be supplied in the form of "Kinder-Eltern," who become vice-parents to all neglected children and at the same time the friendly counselors of the actual fathers and mothers whom they seek to encourage in the moral and religious training of their children. Thus, in the organization and administration of religious education, as well as in his theory of child nature and nurture, Zinzendorf was a progressive in advance of his time, a kindred spirit of all who understand children and who conceive the problem of religious education in terms of creating for the child a wholesome, stimulating religious environment favorable to a normal development of the spiritual life.

For Discussion

1. What were the advantages of dividing the Moravian community congregation into groups according to age?
2. In what respects was Zinzendorf's system of religious education for the Moravian Church similar to the best systems of church-school instruction today?
3. Where is Herrnhut? What great church gathering of recent years was held there?
4. What do you know about the Easter celebrations of the Moravians in the United States at Bethlehem, Pennsylvania, and Winston-Salem, North Carolina?
5. How did Zinzendorf come to his conception of religious development in children?
6. Is it possible to understand children simply by reading about them? How did Zinzendorf gain his insight into child nature?
7. What do you know about the modern missionary enterprises of the Moravian Church?

St. Benedict

by

LOWELL B. HAZZARD
Pastor, Union Methodist Church
Quincy, Illinois

IN GREAT Rome, the temples had begun to fall to ruin. The Capitol, standing upon its desolate hill, still displayed the sumptuous monuments of the greatest Empire known to history. But the Imperial Palace was a haunted and deserted fortress, the Circus Maximus was grass-grown and filled with rubbish, the vast Baths of the imperial times resembled ruined cities in their vastness and desertion. The costly marbles had already fallen, the mosaic pavements were loose and disjointed, some ancient chairs of light or dark marble and splendid baths of porphyry or alabaster still remained in the painted halls, but most had been carried away. Those which were left were soon shattered and overthrown by falling masonry to be buried for centuries in dust.[1]

But the ruin in the city was only the reflection of the confusion in the Empire as a whole. The barbarian invasions had begun. First there was Alaric, then Attila. "Odoacer, the chief of the Herules, had snatched the purple of the Caesars from the shoulders of Augustulus in 476, but disdained himself to put it on."[2] In 489 came Theodoric and the Ostrogoths, and in 493 Theodoric slew Odoacer with his own hand and became ruler of Italy.[3] "Confusion, corruption, despair, and death were everywhere; social dis-

[1] Condensed from Gregorovius, Ferdinand. *Rome in the Middle Ages.* London, George Bell, 1902, vol. II, pp. 1-2.

[2] Montalembert, C. F. R. de. *Monks of the West.* Boston, Noonan, 1860, p. 306.

[3] Butler, Cuthbert. *Benedictine Monachism.* New York, Longmans, Green, 1924, p. 4.

memberment seemed complete."[4] Darkness was falling, and where was the way out of that darkness?

EARLY YEARS OF BENEDICT

Somewhere around the year 500, a youth of perhaps eighteen or twenty years might have been seen making his way out of Rome westward toward the upper waters of the Anio. He had been born in Nursia, a little village of the Sabine highlands, the son of a well-to-do burgher of that village. He had been sent to Rome to pursue there the studies of a liberal education,[5] but he had been disgusted and horrified at the general licentiousness of the city and the dissolute lives of his companions; he had perhaps also been in love, and now, as St. Gregory, his first biographer, tells us, "He withdrew the foot he had just placed in the entry to the world; and despising the pursuit of letters, and abandoning his father's home and property, desiring to please God alone, he determined to become a monk."

He was accompanied at first by his faithful nurse, and finding in the little town of Efide a group of people who listened with sympathy to his sorrows and aspirations, he listened to their advice and took up his abode in a chamber connected with the church of St. Peter.[6] But the place was too public for Benedict. There was "more of the praise of this world than he could bear,"[7] and flying secretly one night from his nurse, he crossed the hills and entered the wild gorge of the Anio.

On the way he met a monk, named Romanus, who gave him a haircloth shirt and a monk's dress.[8] This monk belonged to a monastery in the mountains, but it was no part of Benedict's plan to enter a monastery. He must be alone. And proceeding on his ascent, he discovered a dark and narrow cave, into which the sun never shone. Here he elected to remain and here Romanus periodically brought him food, abstracted from the monastery table. "As no path led down from the monastery to the cave, the basket of provisions was tied to the end of a long rope, to which a bell was

[4] *Rome in the Middle Ages,* p. 306.

[5] *Benedictine Monachism,* p. 2.

[6] Hodgkin, T. *Italy and Her Invaders.* London, Oxford, 1936, vol. IV, p. 414.

[7] The same, p. 415.

[8] *Monks of the West,* vol. I, p. 309.

also attached, and thus the slowly lowered vessel by its tinkling sound, called the Saint from prayer to food."[9]

The cave where Benedict thus took up his abode is in a place called Subiaco, which by its wild beauty had first attracted the attention of Nero, four centuries before. Here Nero had built him a palace and artificial lakes and baths, but now these Roman works were in ruins and the entire place unfrequented and bare. No one came to disturb his solitude, and among the rugged mountains and the naked rocks,[10] Benedict, according to the pattern of his day, began the culture of his soul.

Some three years later, some shepherds of the neighborhood discovered the cave and saw what they at first supposed to be a wild beast, coiled up among the bushes. Upon examination, they found, however, a man, a holy man, dressed in a garment of skins. They listened eagerly to his preaching, and from that time on he was never in want, the shepherds bringing him food and listening to the message he gave.[11]

From that time, however, he was never alone either. Some monks who lived down the stream, having lost their abbot by death, persuaded him against his judgment to come and be their abbot. The experiment was not a success, for he could not endure their loose ways, and at last they tried to poison his food.[12]

So he returned to Subiaco, where gradually twelve monasteries grew up, each one inhabited by twelve monks.[13] He lived in a thirteenth with a few choice friends, to whom he gave special training.

At this time, too, the nobles of Rome began to bring him their sons for education, and so, in teaching and preaching and work about the monastery, the days went smoothly by. But a neighboring priest, Florentius, becoming inflamed with jealousy, began to make trouble, first by trying to draw away the monks, then by an attempt to murder Benedict, finally by trying to seduce the brothers and even Benedict himself.

---

[9] *Italy and Her Invaders,* p. 416.

[10] Compare with, *Benedictine Monachism,* p. 1.

[11] *Italy and Her Invaders,* p. 418.

[12] The same, p. 420.

[13] *Monks of the West,* p. 311.

At last, therefore, Benedict decided to move once more, and about 520, with a selected band of monks, he migrated southward to the mountain known as Monte Cassino, halfway between Rome and Naples. Here he found an ancient grove of Apollo, which he cut down, turned the temple into a chapel of St. Martin, and established the monastery that was to be his home for the remainder of his life, and the center from which "flowed over Europe streams of religion and civilisation, and culture."[14]

It was probably in the early years at Monte Cassino that he wrote the famous Benedictine Rule, and to that we must now turn.

THE BENEDICTINE RULE

The claim of St. Benedict to fame must always lie in the fact that in a day when the world was in darkness and confusion, and those who might have helped it had fled into solitude where they became "ineffectual dreamers and ascetics,"[15] he envisioned a new kind of monasticism and taught his monks another way. Before Benedict, "the life of the hermits of the Egyptian deserts, with their prolonged fasts and vigils," and their bodily austerities, was looked upon as the highest ideal of the monastic life.[16] St. Benedict had tried that, and he can never be said to have despised it. But when he began to teach disciples, he neither taught them to live in solitude nor to vie with one another in bodily austerities. He wrote "A very little rule for beginners"[17] and based it on community, prayer, and work.

"St. Benedict's monks rose early in the morning—usually about two, but the hour varied with the season of the year." They had had, however, usually not less than eight hours sleep, so this was not such a hardship as it seems. They then repaired to the church for the "night office," which consisted of fourteen Psalms and certain other readings from Scripture, and must have taken from an hour to an hour and a half. It was followed by a break that was devoted to private reading of Scripture, or prayer. The "Matin office" was celebrated at dawn, and "Prime" at sunrise; each took about half

---

[14] *Benedictine Monachism*, p. 9.

[15] Dudden, F. Homer. *Gregory the Great.* New York, Longmans, Green, 1905, vol. II, p. 169.

[16] *Cambridge Medieval History.* New York, Macmillan, 1936, vol. I, pp. 535-536.

[17] *Benedictine Monachism*, p. 25 (quoted from the Rule).

an hour. Prime was followed by work (i.e., field work for most of the monks—or reading, according to the time of year) till dinner, either at twelve or three. In summer, when the night sleep was short, the usual Italian siesta was allowed after dinner. The afternoon was passed in work and reading; vespers or evensong was sung before sunset and followed by the evening meal. Before dark, they assembled once again in the church, and after a few pages had been read, "Compline" was said and they retired to rest in the dusk before there was need of artificial light. On Sundays, there was no work, but the time assigned to church services and reading was longer.[18]

Now this may not seem like a very desirable kind of life to the modern American young people who read this chapter, but before we judge it too harshly, let us consider some of the things that Benedict would say about it.

1. He would say that prayer, by which he would mean not so much private prayer as "the celebration of the office," is a very large part of the "work of God." Indeed, he calls it all of the "work of God" ("opus Dei" is his name for it), the most important service that the monk can render. The monastery was a court where perpetual praise was to be offered to God. "The Declarations of the English Congregation say that 'our primary duty is to carry out on earth what the angels do in heaven,' " and Benedict would doubtless have agreed with this.[19]

2. He would say that aside from prayer, the best offering that a man can make to God is the offering of useful labor, and any useful labor was appropriate for the Benedictines. Work on the farm and in the garden, work in the kitchen and bakehouse and shop, literary work, work of preaching to the peasants, or teaching the boys who increasingly were sent to the Benedictine schools—all these were a part of the service of God.

3. Finally, he would say that men need the discipline that comes from living together under a rule. The eremitical life is not for many, but life together is the normal life, and for the good of our souls we need to learn to be obedient. The monastery is under the

---

[18] This description of the Benedictine day is taken from the *Cambridge Medieval History,* vol. I, pp. 537-538.

[19] *Benedictine Monachism,* pp. 29-32.

absolute rule of the abbot, who is to be obeyed in all things. But the abbot is not an absolute monarch. In important matters he must ask the counsel of the whole monastery—on lesser matters, of the elders—and he must always remember that for the souls of all in his care, he must render account to God.

Possibly Benedict was not so wrong as we might suppose. Possibly an age which had nearly forgotten God needed communities of honest and earnest men scattered through it, where God was hourly remembered and worshiped. Possibly an age of confusion needed nothing more than simple, self-forgetful labor, down at the foundations of society, draining swamps, planting gardens, felling forests, learning again that work belongs not to slaves but is the privilege of free men. Possibly an age that was in chaos needed the example of discipline, of men who sought not their own, but submitted themselves to rule, and preferred not their own but each his neighbor's good. But Benedict did not do it to serve his time. He did it to save his soul and the souls of those who came to him—which is another example of the fact that often the best way to serve one's generation is to go searching for God oneself.

BENEDICT'S LAST DAYS

The days at Monte Cassino were uneventful, so far as outer circumstances go. We catch an occasional glimpse of the venerable abbot, quiet, gentle, dignified, strong, and peace-loving. We see him with his monks in the church, at their reading, sometimes in the fields, more commonly in his cell, where frequent messengers find him "weeping silently at his prayers," and in the night hours, standing at the window of his cell in the tower offering up his prayers to God, and often sitting outside the door of his cell or "before the gates of the monastery, reading upon a book."[20]

Often he must have watched from his mountain top the Roman and Gothic armies in the plain below, as they marched and countermarched through the land, spreading havoc and desolation around them,[21] and one day as he sat thus, the Gothic king, Totila, on his way to the siege of Naples in 542, approached the abbot. "But when

[20] "Benedict," *Catholic Encyclopedia.*

[21] *Benedictine Monachism,* p. 9.

he saw him sitting afar off he did not dare to come close, but cast himself upon the ground. Then when the man of God had twice or thrice said to him 'Rise,' but still he did not dare raise himself from the earth, Benedict, the servant of Jesus Christ, condescended himself to approach the prostrate King and cause him to arise. He rebuked him for his past deeds, and in a few words told him all that should come to pass. When he had heard these words, the King, vehemently terrified, asked for his prayers and withdrew. Not long afterwards he entered Rome, and crossed to Sicily. But in the tenth year of his reign, he lost his kingdom and his life."[22]

Within a year, probably, Benedict was dead. He had a beloved sister, Scholastica, whom he met only once a year. And on a certain day they had met as was their custom. When evening came, Scholastica said, "I pray thee, do not leave me tonight, but let us speak of the joys of heaven till the morning."

"What sayest thou, my sister?" answered Benedict. "On no account can I remain out of the monastery."

Scholastica bent her head, and when she raised it again, a violent storm began, rain, lightning, and thunder, so that Benedict could not go out. "May God pardon thee, my sister," said Benedict, "but what hast thou done?"

"I prayed thee," she answered, "and thou wouldst not listen to me; then I prayed God and he heard me. Go now if thou canst and return to thy monastery."

Benedict resigned himself against his will to remain, and they passed the rest of the night in spiritual conversation. Three days later Benedict had a vision in which he saw his sister entering heaven under the form of a dove.

He survived her only forty days. Six days before his death he ordered his grave to be dug. After this he was seized with a sharp attack of fever that daily grew worse. On the sixth day he asked his disciples to carry him into the church, he received the sacrament, and then, leaning upon the arms of his disciples, but standing, and with his arms raised to heaven, he died in the attitude of prayer.

The same day two of his disciples, one in Monte Cassino and the

[22] Gregory, quoted in *Italy and Her Invaders*, pp. 433-434.

other in a distant monastery, saw the same vision. A pathway, gleaming with innumerable fires, stretched eastward from Benedict's cell up to heaven. Above stood a man of venerable aspect and radiant countenance who asked them if they knew what that pathway was which they beheld. They answered, "No," and he replied, "This is the path by which Benedict, beloved of God, hath ascended up to heaven."[23]

So we take leave of Benedict, the founder of western monasticism, surrounded by myth and legend, and the adoration of his disciples.

AND NOW, WHAT OF IT?

And now, what of it? Modern Protestant America, reading a life like this, is apt to sniff and say, "There is nothing here for us." But let us not be too sure of that. Here are the testimonies of two men to the permanent value of Benedict's work. Gregorovius, the author of *Rome in the Middle Ages,* says, "The high-minded Benedict collected within his republic of holy men, all the religious energies of that evil time, and as a law-giver gave them shape. It was his desire to realise the Christian theory of obedience to the moral law, to put in practice the teachings of humility and love, of self-renunciation and moral freedom, and finally to establish a communion of property. The greatness of his order consists in his having shown that these principles are not vain ideals, but can be truly carried out; and if we desire to pay a well-deserved tribute to his system, we may say that in a barbarous age, when brutal egoistic passions governed mankind, it was able to oppose to them the example of a community of active, self-denying men. The Benedictines became the teachers of agriculture, handicrafts, arts and learning, thus conferring an everlasting service on mankind."[24]

And Montalembert, author of *Monks of the West,* says: "The results of Benedict's work were immense. In his lifetime, as after his death, the sons of the noblest races in Italy, and the best of the converted barbarians, came in multitudes to Monte Cassino. They came out again, and descended from it to spread themselves all over the West—missionaries and husbandmen, who were soon to

[23] Compare with *Monks of the West,* vol. I, pp. 325-327, and *Italy and Her Invaders,* pp. 435-439.

[24] *Rome in the Middle Ages,* pp. 10-11.

become the doctors and pontiffs, the artists and legislators, the historians and poets of the new world. They went forth to spread peace and faith, light and life, freedom and charity, knowledge and art, the Word of God and the genius of man, the Holy Scriptures and the great works of classical literature, amid the despairing provinces of the destroyed empire, and even into the barbarous regions from which the destruction came forth. Less than a century after the death of Benedict, all that barbarism had won from civilization was reconquered; and more still, his children took in hand to carry the Gospel beyond those limits which had confined the first disciples of Christ. After Italy, Gaul, and Spain had been retaken from the enemy, Great Britain, Germany, and Scandinavia were in turn invaded, conquered and incorporated into Christendom. The West was saved. A new empire was founded. A new world began."[25]

The most fruitful life is often not the most active life. For sometimes an activist civilization gets to living so much upon the surface of things that it has need of men who will stop and dig in, down deep to where the fountains of living water are, and bring up water for thirsty souls. Civilization needs its thinkers and its saints to keep it from becoming superficial and vain.

And sometimes when things are going very wrong in the world and there seems nothing men can do to stop them, when the economic and political life of the world is in the hands of wicked men, or so confused that even good men cannot keep it from careening to bad ends, more power than we would suppose can be wielded by groups of men who in their living can give an example of the way society ought to be. It was Jesus who first talked about the leaven, and more than once in the history of the world, a very little leaven of good has been found to leaven the whole lump.

Finally, as Montalembert points out, when men do get hold of the fundamental truth of God, and set themselves to teach it, one burning soul setting another on fire, from that center where truth is preached or taught, healing streams flow out which in time can transform a world. Even yet we feel the results of the work of this young man who fled from the world to the cave at Subiaco, with

[25] *Monks of the West*, p. 344.

no other thought in his mind than the desire to please God alone.[26] "To take an illustration from St. Benedict's own beloved Subiaco, the work of his disciples has been like one of the great aqueducts of the valley of the Anio—sometimes carried underground for centuries through the obscurity of unremembered existences, sometimes emerging to the daylight and borne high upon the arcade of noble lives, but equally through all its course bearing the precious streams of ancient thought from the far-off halls of time into the humming and crowded cities of modern civilisation."[27]

Many of us do not see much good in monks. But in the quiet places where men meet God and great ideas come to birth, often the greatest work of the world is done.

For Discussion

1. Was the young Benedict wise or foolish when he fled from a wicked world to save his own soul?
2. Is it possible for young people, who have not developed a deep and rich life within, to do much toward building a new world?
3. What do you think of Benedict's idea that prayer is one of the best ways to serve God? Wouldn't the monks be better occupied in working more than in praying so much?
4. In the present time of confusion, what would you think of small groups of men banding themselves together to live by the principles, which the world ought to follow, but will not?
5. Does Montalembert's tribute to the work of Benedict suggest to you any way besides that of military conquest by which a conquered people can reconquer their conquerors? What do you think of the idea—for China, say?
6. Have we discovered any great truths, which burn so in our lives that they might set others on fire and so ultimately save the world?

SCRIPTURE

The parables of the mustard seed and the leaven. Matt. 13: 31-33.

---

[26] *Benedictine Monachism*, p. 8.
[27] *Italy and Her Invaders*, vol. IV, pp. 441-442.

HYMN

"Welcome, happy morning"—an Easter hymn of the sixth century—(St. Benedict's century). Found in *Hymnal for American Youth,* 117; *New Hymnal for American Youth,* 130; *Methodist Hymnal,* 161.

POEM

This is the conclusion of a poetic tribute to St. Benedict by the poet, Mark, an early Benedictine:

> Christ's mount art thou, thus to command the rest.
> Beneath thy feet Cassino lowered its crest.
> To let thee find a dwelling on its crown,
> It bows its head and smooths its roughness down;
> Lest men should tire who seek thy high abode,
> Winds round its sides a gently-sloping road.
> Yet justly does the mountain honour thee,
> For thou hast made it rich and fair to see.
> Its barren sides by thee are gardens made,
> Its naked rocks with fruitful vineyards laid,
> The crags admire a crop and fruit not theirs,
> The wild wood now a bounteous harvest bears.
> E'en so our barren deeds to fruit thou trainest,
> Upon our arid hearts pure water rainest.
> Turn now to fruit the evil thorns, I pray,
> That vex the stupid breast of Mark alway.[28]

PRAYER

A prayer of the fiftn century church:

"Almighty God, who alone canst order the unruly wills and affections of sinful men; grant unto thy people that they may love the thing which thou commandest, and desire that which thou dost promise; that so, among the sundry and manifold changes of the world, our hearts may surely there be fixed, where true joys are to be found; through Jesus Christ, our Lord. Amen."[29]

For Further Reading

McCann, Dom Justin. *St. Benedict.* New York, Sheed and Ward, 1937.

[28] Quoted from McCann, Dom Justin. *St. Benedict.* New York, Sheed and Ward, 1937, p. 267.

[29] Quoted from Noyes, M. P. *Prayers for Services.* New York, Scribner, 1934, p. 114.

This is the newest book on St. Benedict, and should be read by all who desire to understand his work.

Montalembert. *Monks of the West.* Boston, Noonan, 1860, vol. I, book IV.

Gregorovius. *Rome in the Middle Ages.* London, Bell, 1902, vol. II, ch. I.

Hodgkin, T. *Italy and Her Invaders.* London, Oxford, 1936, vol. IV, ch. XVI.

Dudden, F. Homer. *Gregory the Great.* New York, Longmans, Green, 1905, vol. II, ch. IX.

Butler, Cuthbert. *Benedictine Monachism.* New York, Longmans, Green, 1924.

Cambridge Medieval History. New York, Macmillan, 1936, vol. I, ch. XVIII.

Articles on "Benedict" in *Catholic Encyclopedia* and *Encyclopedia Britannica.*

St. Francis of Assisi

by

W. D. SCHERMERHORN
Emeritus Professor of Church History
Garrett Biblical Institute

O most high, almighty, good Lord God, to thee belong praise, glory, honor and all blessing!

Praised be my Lord God with all his creatures and specially our brother the sun, who brings us the day and who brings us the light; fair is he and he shines with a very great splendor; O Lord, he signifies to us, thee!

Praised be my Lord for our sister the moon, and for the stars, the which he hath set clear and lovely in heaven.

Praised be my Lord for our brother the wind, and for air and cloud, calms and all weather by the which thou upholdest life in all creatures.

Praised be the Lord for our sister water, who is very serviceable unto us and humble and precious and clean.

Praised be my Lord for our brother fire, through whom thou givest us light in the darkness; and he is bright and pleasant and very mighty and strong.

Praised be my Lord for our mother the earth, the which doth sustain and keep us, and bringeth forth divers fruits and flowers of many colors and grass.

Praised be my Lord for all those who pardon one another for his love's sake, and they who endure weakness and tribulation; blessed are they who peaceably shall endure, for thou, O most Highest, shall give them a crown.

Praised be the Lord for my sister, the death of the body, from which no man escapeth. Woe to him who dieth in mortal sin!

Blessed are they who are found walking by thy most holy will, for the second death shall have no power to do them harm.

Praise ye and bless the Lord, and give thanks unto him and serve him with great humility.[1]

FRANCIS of Assisi was born in 1182 and died 1226; thus, he belongs to the Middle Ages, so far as his dates are concerned. But, really, he belongs to all subsequent history. He was the son of Bernardoni, a cloth merchant of somewhat generous means. The social status of a mere merchant was not regarded as high, but the ability of father and son to spend freely easily threw them into the companionship of those who were regarded as socially superior. Many tales have been told of the early life of Francis. The facts seem to be that he was of a very sprightly temperament and found his satisfactions in ways that were regarded by his contemporaries as somewhat "fast." He was not completely deaf to the call of a more serious life, but for the most part he gave himself to sport, with little or no restraint.

One can scarcely blame him for his giddy life. There was much to invite and little to restrain. It was the time of the troubadours and of the reign of chivalry. The gay singers and the glorious knights challenged the admiration of youth. The Church was not vigorous enough in its spirituality to lay very clamant call upon adolescence, full of life and vigor. The feudal organization of society had made the Church a part of its great network. The bishops were, in many cases, feudal lords with large holdings and much patronage. They managed estates that to our day seem almost unbelievably large. It has been estimated that during the feudal period the richest clergy would possess from 75,000 to 140,000 acres of land, the medium rich from 25,000 to 50,000 acres, and the poorest from 5,000 to 7,500 acres. The revenue from these lands is estimated at from $85,000 to $225,000 for the richest, the medium from $28,000 to $56,000 and the poorest from $5,000 to $14,000. One of the pathetic aspects, also, of the monasteries, whose monks had taken the vows of poverty, was that as institutions, by inheritance, by gifts, and by their earnings, they became immensely wealthy—so much so, indeed, as to embarrass the princes in whose realms they had their location.

---

[1] "The Canticle of the Sun," by Francis of Assisi, translation as found in Matthew Arnold, *Essays in Criticism,* Second Series, New York, Macmillan, 1883.

The parish priests, although not rich, were unlearned and superstitious. They gave themselves to the miracle-mongering of the period. They were not expected to preach. Their task seemed chiefly to perform the miracle attendant upon the celebration of the Mass and to manage such "relics" and other means of magic as were in the reach of their churches. All nature was peopled with spirits, and it was the work of the clergy to control these creatures rather than to promote piety among their parishioners. The high offices of the Church came to be sought by the nobility, were often purchased, and were filled by men regarded as above the common people. The only defense society had against the establishment of a hereditary class, who might even threaten the rule of kings and emperors, was the insistence upon clerical celibacy, so that at the death of each bishop or abbot the new incumbent had to make a fresh start in the matters of wealth and prestige.

It is true that there were certain reforming groups in the Church, and many protesting sects who opposed the abuses of the Church. Among the better known are the Waldensians, who were called "the Poor Men of Lyons" and the Cathari. They struck out with terrific vigor against the immense wealth of the Church in the face of the very great poverty of the masses. Various monastic groups, which had begun with high professions, had become rich and were deteriorating. In a society such as this, obviously there was little to invite this sincere, vigorous, and open-minded son of an Italian merchant to religion.

Francis, when he was not out with his young friends, helped in his father's shop, and he loved the business. He was musical, and had an interest in singing. He developed those habits of courtesy attending the observances of chivalry. Thus, his life was not wholly given up to frivolity. When religion had its opportunity, a real man gave answer. One of the stories of his early life is that once, when Francis was in his father's shop, a beggar entered and, in the name of God, asked an alms. Francis sent him rudely away. Then, thinking upon it, he said: "Had any one come in the name of a prince or baron, asking a favor, how quickly I should have granted it. But this man came in the name of the Most High, and I turned him away." Leaving his customers, Francis ran after the beggar and insisted upon making amends. His father, learning of it, was not pleased. He was willing to pay the bills of a son to make him popular with distinguished companions, but he had slight interest in large gifts to beggars.

Francis came into touch with certain reformers of his time who insisted upon communal ownership of property. There were several such sects in France, and their influence penetrated into Italy. Also, there is evidence that Germanic custom was very generous in the matter of landholdings. The monastic and other Christian organizations had noted the various references to common ownership in the Bible, and so Francis had this teaching in his background.

Francis joined in the unhappy struggles of his time between rival Italian cities and in the wars of the Popes against the Germanic princes. He saw his own city thrown into ruins and rebuilt, and with his fellow citizens rejoiced when Assisi attained importance enough to become virtually self-governing. But the wars had their effect upon Francis. Upon his return, although he tried to enter upon the usual social round, he became ill; in the weakness incident upon convalescence, he became more contemplative and quiet. Here his conversion seems to have its beginning.

His parents encouraged him to join an expedition to fight for Innocent III in southern Italy. Their wealth easily made him one of the most glamorous knights in the army. But it seems that on the very night of departure, he had a vision directing him to return to Assisi. His return, weak and ill, was a great disappointment to his parents. From this time he seems to have turned further away from his former habits, for they had now but slight attraction for him. He became restless and longing.

On occasion he entered a grotto in the country near Assisi, where in solitude he gave himself to prayer and heart-searching. His friends missed him from the feasts. They chided him with the expectation of taking a wife, and he answered them cryptically that he was planning to take a wife more beautiful, more rich, more pure than they were able to imagine. But inasmuch as he finally ceased to join them, they accepted the situation. His real friends now became the beggars to whom formerly he had given scant attention. Sabatier points out that the beggars of St. Francis' day were not morally destitute, but were chiefly poor because of bad harvests and sickness. What they needed in their indigence was sympathy rather than simply alms. This, Francis was able to give them. His father became more and more dissatisfied with the distribution of their property to the poor. Gradually Francis came to a devotion to religion which was plainly to shut out everything else.

The completion of his conversion was in the humble chapel called St. Damien, in a suburb of Assisi, served by a priest who had scarcely enough to eat. The altar was of crude masonry. The reredos was only a crucifix. This crucifix had an expression of calm and gentleness, rather than the usual one of pain and anguish, and the eyes, instead of being closed to the weight of suffering, looked upon the worshiper more in the spirit of invitation than of the proclamation of death. It was at this altar that Francis found the marvel, the supreme crisis of his life. Both within and about him, he felt that Jesus claimed his life; and the heart of the man, which had formerly sought satisfactions in the gaities of the world, now found its complete triumph in Christ. From this point he is certain that Christ is his, and, what is equally important, that he belongs absolutely to Christ.

At once the choice for a manner of life had to be made. The delights that had come to him in solitude might have led him to choose a life of contemplation. Instead, Francis believed himself called to a life of such activities as Jesus himself would have undertaken had he been living in the age of Francis. The first move was to repair the little chapel in which his vision had come. He gave the priest all the money he had, he sold his horse and the gaudy garments which he possessed, together with such packages of cloth as were his, and in full purpose to leave his father's house and business, he turned the entire proceeds over to the priest and asked permission to join in his life at the chapel. At first the priest feared that the money belonged to Bernardoni, and he hesitated to take it, but finally it became the property of the chapel.

The father sought to compel his son to return, but Francis, in great joy, remained. Clothed in such meager rags as were left to him, on the streets he was hailed as a madman, and the children are said to have flung stones and mud upon him. The father brought Francis before the courts of Assisi, but the consuls ruled that inasmuch as he had now become a servant of the Church, he did not come under their jurisdiction but rather must be judged by the Church. When Francis appeared before the episcopal court, he simply said that he had determined to make Jesus Christ the Lord of his life. He purposed fully to serve God. Having taken off every stitch of clothing, he rolled it in a bundle and appeared nude before the court. He gave over the clothing he was carrying along with such little money as he had. He announced that up to this time he had called Bernardoni "father," but that henceforth he purposed to serve God only. Therefore, he was returning all that Bernardoni had ever given him, and henceforth he desired to say "Our Father who art in heaven."

Bernardoni took the clothes and money and walked out of the court, without compassion. The Bishop was forced to throw his mantle around Francis to cover his nakedness. Thus violently did Francis undertake the life of devotion. With a garment given him by charitable observers, he returned in joy to St. Damien.

It was on this journey that he had the well-known experience with the lepers, who had hitherto always been very repulsive to him. Tradition has it that he washed and wiped their sores, and one story even has it that he exchanged garments with them. At least, he found that the love he now had overcame the fears to which he had been accustomed, and he entered upon a life of complete bravery. Francis refused to share the food of the priest of the chapel, believing that he should either earn or else beg his food. As he passed through the streets of Assisi asking for something to eat, his father, seeing him, cursed him. Francis replied by saying, "I will give you the sign of the cross." Thus, Francis began his life of complete separation to his ideal. He showed no signs of grief or solemnity. In fact, he was as jolly or even more so than in the days of his earlier hilarity, and his personality was even more charming. He went about preaching the Gospel, and the people gladly supplied him with food. Soon, his life of devotion attracted the attention of others who, like himself, were sick of worldliness, and they asked permission to join him. In every case Francis pledged them by the Scripture that had so powerfully influenced his own decision: "These twelve Jesus sent forth, and charged them, saying, Go not into any way of the Gentiles, and enter not into any city of the Samaritans: but go rather to the lost sheep of the house of Israel. And as ye go, preach, saying, The kingdom of heaven is at hand.

Heal the sick, raise the dead, cleanse the lepers, cast out demons: freely ye received, freely give. Get you no gold, nor silver, nor brass in your purses: no wallet for your journey, neither two coats, nor shoes, nor staff: for the laborer is worthy of his food."[2] In the beginning, there was no other rule.

Manifestly, a group of this sort would fly in the face of a time-serving church. Francis and his companions had no house that could be called their own. Instead of asking to be served, they went about among the people, joining them in their daily tasks as well as preaching and singing along the way. In the "Christian" world, where Christianity consisted so largely in formal sacraments and creeds, they were exhibiting a Christianity of loving deeds. They would love all, they would serve all, they would never avenge a wrong, they would own no property, they would spend and be spent in simply doing good. Although this movement was an embarrassment to a formal Church, it aroused great enthusiasm among the common people. Increasingly, others asked to join the number of the friars, and many of the applicants were from the common walks of life, which was in contrast with the lofty pretensions of the clerical higher-ups. Even the established monasteries, with their properties and security, either opposed or else sneered at the idea of absolute poverty. It soon became evident to Francis that if he and his comrades were to escape blotting out, he would need the approval of the Pope. So, with eleven others of his followers, he went to Rome, making simply the one request that he might organize a society within the Church devoted to the one task of being like Christ. Certainly it would have been a sad irony if the Pope, who was called the "vicar of Christ," had refused such a request. Yet he saw that it involved a struggle in the Church and gave consent grudgingly. Later the wisdom of his permission was seen when it became evident that this new "order," devoted to poverty and to preaching, became the bulwark of the papacy against the more radical reformers who would split the Church.

Thus, the summer of 1210 marked the official beginning of what is now known as the Franciscan Movement. Francis had no purpose that it should bear his name. He and his companions sought for a

[2] Matthew 10: 5-10.

suitable title, and finally decided to call themselves "Minores," meaning "little ones," and thus expressed the humility they hoped would always characterize the members of their order. They came chiefly from the humbler walks of life; they had renounced those conditions and emoluments that make men famous; they proposed to serve in utter poverty and not to rule; they believed that the name "Minores" would help keep them to their purpose. There is no room in this sketch to tell completely either of St. Francis or of the movement that grew up in his following. We shall consider only certain features:

The habitual *joyousness* of the friars and their *appreciation of nature* were conspicuous features. Wherever they went, they sang. They had no tale of woe, but rather Good News, which they told on every possible occasion. In a different way, but as truly as ever, Francis was jolly, even hilarious. He counted himself "God's Troubadour." He and his brethren had no quarrel with nature. They loved the earth, the trees, the flowers, the clouds, the sun, moon, and stars. Their utter friendliness to all beasts and birds was met by returning friendliness. From this comes the tradition of the birds singing to St. Francis, and of his preaching to them. Doubtless he did enjoy an intimacy with these creatures that can come only to those who are always kind to them.

St. Francis had no hostility to the *Church*. He had the blessing of the Pope, and although he came into conflict with some of the priests and with some of the more formal monastic orders, he recognized that with the real Church of Christ he had no quarrel. He never became a priest, but only a deacon; thus, he and his fellow friars might almost be called a lay movement. They doubtless provided a satisfactory religious refuge for many who would otherwise have separated from the Church and joined its enemies.

The *poverty* of these friars, in the beginning, was absolute. They sought to apply the vow literally and completely. St. Francis is said even to have rebuked a brother for ownership of a breviary. These preachers went forth two-by-two. They entered the fields of the farmers and helped them with their work, singing and preaching as they labored. At evening they would take such food as was offered, sleep in a haystack or hedgerow, and pass along to tell the Good News and to live it as they went. They refused to take any money gifts. They hoped that not only the individuals might remain free from any constraint due to possessions, but that the order itself might remain in poverty like its founder.

They had as headquarters an abandoned leper-house that had been loaned to them. When away from this center, they could build themselves booths of leaves or straw. But as the order developed, there arose a group who believed that the society could best serve if it would receive gifts, have a home, and be able to distribute from its center. This led to intense struggle among the brethren, and for years rival groups in the Franciscan camp contended regarding the principle of institutional as well as individual poverty. The fact is that, although St. Francis was himself in favor of utter renunciation of property, there did arise a Franciscan order that has its properties and the solidity coming from such investments.

Some think that it was in the laceration of spirit over this matter, and while he was in prayer, feeling almost that his very ideals were being crucified, that he experienced what is known as the reception of the "*Stigmata* of Christ." The tradition is that while in intense prayer there appeared to him a heavenly vision in which a seraph flew toward him and bathed his spirit in ineffable joy. In the vision a cross appeared, and upon the cross was the seraph. The vision so deeply moved him that it left, in his hands, on his feet, and in his side, marks resembling the wounds of Christ. Much controversy has arisen with reference to this account. Our age is miracle-shy. Sabatier, in a lengthy appendix, gives the testimony of those who claim to have seen the very marks, both during his life and after his death. There are some who contend that no miracle need be posited, but that the relation of body and spirit is such that it could have naturally occurred. St. Paul claimed to bear in his body "the marks of Jesus."[3] In over a hundred cases, one or more of the stigmata of the cross are stated to have been reproduced in the persons of fervent Christians. It is interesting to read the accounts of Sabatier[4] or the article by Cowan in *Encyclopædia of Religion and Ethics.*[5]

A very important by-product of the preaching movement was the utter freedom and unconstraint that furnished a growing-plot for the

[3] Galatians 6: 17.
[4] Sabatier, Paul. *Life of St. Francis of Assisi.* New York, Scribner, 1916.
[5] Edited by James Hastings. New York, Scribner.

scholarship needed in the new universities that were at this very time springing up. It will be news to many to know that both the Franciscans and their kindred preaching-order, the Dominicans, included among their number very famous medieval scholars—among them Roger Bacon, Thomas Aquinas, Bonaventura, Albertus Magnus, and Duns Scotus. These men were not so subject to outward constraints, and were so released in mind and spirit, that they became the great thinkers of their time.

The Franciscans were great *missionaries*. They believed that they were sent to recover "the lost sheep of the house of Israel." To this end Francis made a trip to Syria to try to recover to the Church those who there were not in harmony with Catholicism. The missionaries labored also with those who threatened to withdraw from the Church. Their further attempts took them into France, Britain, Germany, and Spain. Francis went with the crusading armies and suffered himself to be taken prisoner, in order that he might preach to the Moslems. He was given a favorable audience with the Sultan. He was deeply shocked by the coarse lives of many of the Christian armies and found his preaching handicapped by this. Certain of the friars were massacred by the Turks and thus crowned with martyrdom their preaching of the Cross. To our own day the Franciscans have a deep interest in Missions, particularly to the Moslems. Americans should be interested to know that Columbus, in 1493, was accompanied by Franciscan friars.

It was only natural that the *women* of Italy, hearing the preaching and seeing the lives of these earnest men, should want to have a part in the movement. Francis very early received as one member of his order a young woman named Clara. She was given a little cloister, which was prepared for her and for her younger sister, who soon followed her. Her mother and a second sister later joined them, and there grew up around this beginning a distinct group within the Franciscan movement, known as the "Poor Clares." This order continues to our day, with houses on both sides of the Atlantic.

One more very important feature is what might be termed a *lay section* of the order. Many who were touched by the preaching of these friars were unable completely to leave their life among the men of business or trade. For these, there was organized a movement called "Tertiaries," although the name probably was not given them until after Francis' death. Although these labored in the usual vocations of life, they held all their possessions as belonging to God, and kept only such as was needful for use, freely investing the balance in some form of Christian service. They were, therefore, not required absolutely to renounce property, or to wear a habit, or to take on fastings and vigils impossible to the life of daily toil. They were bound by simple vows and joined to a great order challenging them to a life of deepest devotion to religion.

The study will close with two quotations, the one providing an estimate and the other offering a challenge. The first is by Matthew Arnold:[6] "He (Francis) fitted religion to popular use. He founded the most popular body of ministers of religion that has ever existed in the Church. He transformed monachism by uprooting the stationary monk, delivering him from the bondage of property and sending him as a mendicant friar to be a stranger and a sojourner, not in the wilderness, but in the most crowded haunts of men, to console them and to do them good. This popular instinct of his is at the bottom of his famous marriage with poverty. Poverty and suffering are the condition of the people, the multitude, the immense majority of mankind; and it was toward this *people* that his soul yearned."

The challenge is from Sabatier: "Even now if in these dying days of the nineteenth century, preachers would go forth beside themselves with love, sacrificing themselves for each and all as in the old days their Master did, the miracle would be repeated again."[7]

For Discussion

1. May prophetic and reforming spirits better achieve their hopes by remaining in a church largely corrupt and unsympathetic or by separating and forming a new organization? Compare St. Francis and Martin Luther.
2. What are the points of comparison between St. Francis and his friars in the midst of the Crusades and modern missionaries and preachers, set in the wars and preparations for war of our time?

---

[6] From *Essays in Criticism,* Second Series, New York, Macmillan, 1925.
[7] From *Life of Francis of Assisi.*

3. What of Sabatier's statement? Do you agree that such a movement would even now command a popular following? Why?
4. What about the monastic ideal? Is there a place in Protestantism for anything resembling any part of St. Francis' movement? If so, what?
5. "The hope of gain is a necessary incentive to progress." Do such personalities as St. Francis disprove this? Discuss.
6. In striking at unrestricted private ownership, the Franciscans believed they could eliminate the vicious control of power. Would that be true in our own day? Could the Christian Church conceivably lead in such a matter? At what cost?

For Further Reading

Coulton, Z. G. *Life in the Middle Ages.* New York, Macmillan, 1930.

No better book can be read for "orientation." It is made up entirely of source-documents translated from medieval materials.

Thompson, James Westfall. *Economic and Social History of the Middle Ages.* New York, Appleton-Century, 1931.

A good popular history of the period.

Scudder, Vida. *Brother John, a Tale of the First Franciscans.* Boston, Little, Brown, 1927.

A notable popular work in the field that gives a penetrating study of the inner struggles of the order concerning property.

————. "Prophetic Elements in the Franciscan Movement." *Christendom,* Vol. III, No. 3.

Sabatier, Paul. *St. Francis of Assisi.* New York, Scribner, 1916.

The standard biography. It is thoroughly done, has ample documentation, and adds special studies of disputed matters such as the "stigmata." Moreover, it has literary charm and generosity of spirit that leave little to be desired.

Horace Bushnell

by

A. J. W. Myers

Head of Department of Religious Education
Hartford School of Religious Education

Litchfield County, Connecticut, a rural county, is famous because of the people it produced. H. Clay Trumbull's pamphlet, *Litchfield County, Connecticut,* has as a subtitle, "One Rural County's Contribution to the Nation's Power and Fame."[1] The remarkable list of people sent out into the nation's life from this small place is an inspiration to all rural communities. Here Horace Bushnell was born in 1802. He graduated at Yale College in 1827. In 1833 he married Mary Apthorp—"a union of rare helpfulness and mutual sympathy"—and became minister of the North Congregational Church in Hartford, where he remained until, on account of failing health, he resigned in 1853. He continued working hard, writing and publishing, until his death in 1876.

It is well to remember that at this time Wordsworth, Coleridge, and Southey had discovered nature and begun a new movement in English poetry, and that Scott and Dickens were already famous. Science was beginning to disturb some old theological doctrines. The anti-slavery agitation rose to white heat. The United States' Civil War was fought. Woman's suffrage became a bitter political question. Manufacturing was becoming a major industry, and factory towns were building. These indicate some of the changes that were taking place in many directions. The character of any leading person is pretty well revealed in the basic faith by which he lives and by his attitude in major issues in his own time. This brief

[1] Philadelphia, The Sunday School Times Co., 1902, title page.

sketch of Bushnell's life will enable the reader to test him by these standards.

Bushnell was a prophet. He saw truth. He had the intuition of a poet and cast his thought into striking words. He apparently had some of the qualities of the saint—the courage that knows no fear and the gentle, healing spirit that finds its strength in God.

Perhaps the best way to get some conception of Horace Bushnell is to examine his attitude and work in several larger fields of influence.

THE FORWARD LOOK

Bushnell was not afraid of the future. He did not lean backwards for fear that if he let go of the old there would be nothing solid left. He looked forward joyously to fuller truth, believing that God was leading on. Devotion to truth was a passion.

He was one of the first among religious leaders to welcome the conception of nature revealed in the new school of English poets and in the discoveries of science. His book, *Nature and the Supernatural* (1858), is, in general, in line with liberal religious thought today. This forward look and open-mindedness to new truth is revealed in almost every area of life.

Young people, as well as old, may be afraid of life. If they are, the defense attitude develops. To change is always difficult. It means losing some of one's sense of security and at-homeness. Instead of changing, one fights to retain the old and builds up reasons to support his position—a process called rationalization. One of the problems of life is to know how to stand firmly for essentials and at the same time be fluid and growing and hospitable to new ideas.

Bushnell accomplished this even in regard to himself. In the early controversies in which he was involved, he loved the battle and wrote devastatingly in criticism of his opponents; but, seeing this was not the best, he resolved never to do so again, and under bitterest provocation kept this resolve. "He that ruleth his spirit (is better) than he that taketh a city."

Just after he had published a two-volume work, a friend asked him if he had reached finality. "He replied: 'By no means. If I got fresh light tomorrow I would recall these books, whatever the publisher might say.' "[2] Self-criticism of one's own work and its revision is essential for growth.

It was because he believed that in the discovery of any new truth one was working with God and carrying out his purposes that he thought of himself as "one of God's experimenters."

THE POLITICAL FIELD

1. The question of slavery agitated men's souls and almost split the nation. Extremists on both sides fanned the flames of bitterness. Bushnell was for freeing the slaves, but did not ally himself with the extreme abolitionists. It is exceedingly difficult to live in a time of bitter partisanship and not belong to either party, but take, rather, a strong stand for what is believed to be a better way. Kipling's "If" portrays this vividly.

2. It may be difficult for young people today to conceive of the political turmoil the woman's suffrage question produced. Bushnell had ideas, and his *Woman's Suffrage—The Reform against Nature* is an able analysis of the problem.

3. Roads fascinated him. They are a symbol of communication, of interchange, of friendship. How he would have gloried in our magnificent roads and means of travel today. Without roads, he says, people are savages. This paragraph from an address, "The Day of Roads," gives something of the sweep of his vision: "Beginning at Scotland, the Roman could travel on by post to Antioch, a distance of nearly four thousand miles, interrupted only by the passage of the English Channel and the Hellespont. And it is actually related, as one of the memorabilia of the age, that one Cæsarius went post from Antioch to Constantinople, six hundred and sixty-five miles, in less than six days."[3]

Roads stand for interchange of ideas, for commerce and civilization, for the "road of thought"—or is it merely for speed?

4. There were, and there are still, many theories of government. He gave an address before a learned society on "The True Wealth and Weal of Nations." Philosophers, politicians, and Fourth of July orators discuss it. Bushnell's formula is clear and basic. It is

[2] Myers, A. J. W. *Horace Bushnell and Religious Education.* Boston, Manthorne and Burack, 1937, p. 165.

[3] *Work and Play, or Literary Varieties.* New York, Scribner, 1871, p. 407.

not military power, or natural resources, or extent of territories. "It consists, however, *in the total value of the persons of the people.*"[4]

5. With this point of view there can be no idolatry of a flag or constitution. Thus, it is not surprising that he advocated a change in the constitution and in representation in Congress.

6. After a visit to Europe he wrote a letter to the Pope,[5] Gregory XVI, in which he severely criticized not the "old man" who held the office but the system in which he was entangled. He pleads earnestly for the Church "to renounce *force* as an instrument of religion," to reform the government—"the worst government in Christendom,"[6] the ambitious and greedy priesthood, monopolies, its confessional and police spy systems, its frauds and its "silly trifles that you call *sacred relics.*"[7] He criticizes the pomp and circumstance, the military display of one who claims to be the successor of the humble fisherman Peter and a follower of the lowly Nazarene.

This letter was widely circulated in the United States, Great Britain, and Italy. It was put on the Index Expurgatorius by the Roman church "and specified by proclamation, as one of the seditious publications to be suppressed by the police."[8]

CIVIC MATTERS

Bushnell was a powerful influence for good in the whole life of his city. Several of these areas may be mentioned.

1. He was a great believer in the common school and was ever on the side of its improvement. His influence in creating public opinion in its favor was great when such support could not be taken for granted. The question of teaching religion in the schools was hotly debated. In a notable address entitled "Common Schools," he made these proposals, which form a good basis for discussion today:

"(1) Make the use of the Bible in the Protestant or Douay version optional.

(2) Compile a book of Scripture reading lessons by agreement from both versions.

---

[4] *Work and Play,* p. 51.

[5] *Building Eras in Religion.* New York, Scribner, 1881, pp. 356-385.

[6] The same, p. 360.

[7] The same, p. 370.

[8] The same, p. 356, footnote.

(3) Provide for religious instruction, at given hours or on a given day, by the clergy or qualified teachers, such as the parents may choose.

(4) Prepare a book of Christian morality, distinct from a doctrine of religion or faith, which shall be taught indiscriminately to all the scholars."[9]

2. But he saw clearly even then that knowledge of words alone can never educate. He points out that educated people are called "men of letters." That was all right in the past, because the only knowledge worth having was in books, especially in Greek and Latin and Hebrew. Now, however, "the world itself is . . . *God's classic.*"[10] "There is a far higher wonder-working and a sweeter magic in the spells of the life-power" than in all fables and miracles, "and that with the advantage that these more than romantic wonders are yet true."[11]

He had also made the discovery which many schools and churches have not yet made—that it is experience and not words that educate.

3. The Park River, a small stream, curved around near his church. It spread through the low-lying land, and here were some of the poorest housing conditions in the city. With undaunted persistence he worked to get the city to tear down these slums and create a park sloping up and up to the Capitol. Finally the city council made the decision. It was one of Bushnell's delights to walk in the park and see people enjoying themselves in its grass and flowers and shade. In his last illness he was greatly cheered by receiving word that this lovely open space was to be called Bushnell Park.

4. It is interesting indeed that long before the days of City Planning in this country he gave a remarkable address on "City Plans." His concluding sentence is, "Every village, town, city ought to be continued as a work of art, and prepared for the new age of ornament to come."[12]

---

[9] The same, p. 93.
[10] The same, p. 38.
[11] *Work and Play,* pp. 308-336.
[12] *Building Eras in Religion,* p. 63.

THE CHURCH

Some people are progressive in everything but religion. It was not so with Bushnell.

1. In that day almost every church had a revival annually. In these revivals the aim was to work people up to a fever pitch and get them to "decide for Christ." This was the accepted practice. Indeed, the success of the church was almost identified with the success of the revivals measured by the number of conversions yearly. Bushnell had the great courage to oppose this whole procedure and to deny that revivals were an especial display of God's presence.[13] In response to fervent preaching, singing, and praying, God was supposed to come into the heart as if God had to come "from a state of isolation above, from beyond fixed stars, from an island where he dwells."[14] He held strongly to the position that God is ever in the world and in the human heart. The fact that revivalist campaigns have practically ceased shows how sound was his judgment.

2. It was also a time of great missionary activity. The work was highly organized, and the purpose was to save people from their religion and convert them to Christianity. Bushnell held that this was but a form of conquest, of coercion. He was as thoroughly missionary as anyone, but he claimed that the only way was by "the outpopulating power of Christianity." The way of the Master was by personal contact and love to blow the smoking flax into a flame. "Growth, Not Conquest the True Method of Christian Progress" is the title of this striking sermon.[15]

3. In his books on the Atonement, on the life and work of Christ, and on Nature and the Supernatural, he took a definite stand far in advance of his time and, of course, called down upon himself severe criticism and opposition.

4. But his greatest contribution was in the field of religious education. Many churches taught that every child was born totally depraved and that one could do nothing to save his own soul. God

---

[13] Bushnell, Horace. *Views of Christian Nurture and of Subjects Adjacent Thereto.* Hartford, Edwin Hunt, 1847, p. 145. Trumbull, H. Clay. *Litchfield County, Connecticut,* p. 9.

[14] Myers, *Horace Bushnell and Religious Education,* p. 41.

[15] *Views of Christian Nurture,* p. 147.

alone could do that. And yet each individual was held alone responsible for that about which, by the premises, he could do nothing. Everyone, therefore, had to go through a rather extreme emotional turmoil of conversion. Bushnell, in the face of this accepted doctrine, came out boldly with the assertion "that the child is to grow up a Christian, and never know himself as being otherwise."[16]

This position is as important in religious education as the Magna Charta is in government. He believed in what he called "Christian Nurture" (the title of his most famous book), and showed clearly that this was the belief and practice of the early Christians.

It is difficult perhaps to understand now the terrific storm this produced. For years organized attacks were made on Bushnell and the strongest pressure brought to bear to bring him to trial for heresy. In spite of it all he never wavered. He was never tried, and heresy hunting in New England met a major defeat. What was revolutionary then is now the accepted position of all liberal-minded churches. Truth prevailed over obscurantism.

Now this theory places great responsibility on the home and the Church. If religion is so vitally important for everyday life, the home and Church must provide the best religious education possible for all its people, from the youngest to the oldest. It calls for planning to meet the needs of all, for helping them to experience religious values and not merely to talk about them; it calls for the best leadership.

THE HOME

1. The other great and fundamental institution of civilization and religion is the home. Bushnell held that there is "something like a law of organic connection" between parents and children in the family, and that if the home practices Christian living so that the whole atmosphere is Christian in fact, the children are almost as likely to absorb its spirit as they are its language and customs. There is no doubt in the minds of thoughtful people today that the home stamps itself on children and that the Christian home is the nursery of the Church.

Bushnell grew up in a home of that kind, and that was the char-

[16] The same, p. 6, and Myers, *Horace Bushnell and Religious Education*, p. 49.

acter of his own home. He and his wife and their daughters practiced their religion.[17] The spirit of the home should be happy camaraderie and mutual helpfulness and thoughtfulness.

2. In those days work was one of the household gods. Industry was a mark of respectability and the key to prosperity. Work on farms and factories was often from sunup to sundown if not from candlelight to candlelight. There was little place for play.

One of the most popular hymns was "Work for the Night Is Coming." Of course, it may be said this means work ceaselessly to bring in the Kingdom of God, but it also expresses the generally accepted glorification of work. Note its words:

"Work, for the night is coming, Work thro' the morning hours;
Work, while the dew is sparkling, Work 'mid springing flow'rs;
Work, when the day grows brighter, Work in the glowing sun;
Work, for the night is coming, When man's work is done.

"Work, for the night is coming, Work thro' the sunny noon;
Fill brightest hours with labor, Rest comes sure and soon.
Give ev'ry flying minute Something to keep in store:
Work, for the night is coming, When man works no more.

"Work, for the night is coming, Under the sunset skies;
While their bright tints are glowing, Work, for daylight flies.
Work, 'till the last beam fadeth, Fadeth to shine no more;
Work while the night is dark'ning, When man's work is o'er."

But Bushnell saw the value of play. One of his best-known addresses was entitled "Work and Play."[18] It is of such high literary quality that Charles Dudley Warner included it in his *Library of the World's Best Literature*. Bushnell's prose had a wonderful rhythm and he "so set down his words that they read like a chant and sound like the breaking of waves upon the beach."[19]

"Work," he said, "is activity *for* one end; play, activity *as* an end."[20] Professional sport may be work, not play. He says the

[17] Cheney, Mary Bushnell. *Life and Letters of Horace Bushnell.* New York, Harper, 1880, pp. 139-142. *Horace Bushnell and Religious Education,* pp. 180-183.

[18] *Work and Play,* pp. 9-42.

[19] Warner, Charles Dudley (editor). *Library of the World's Best Literature, Ancient and Modern.* New York, Peale and Hill, 1897, vol. V, p. 2913.

[20] *Views of Christian Nurture,* p. 13.

"pure ideal" is "a state of play." This is found nowhere but in religion "where well doing is its own end and joy."[21] Worship is an end in itself, the joy of fellowship and communion with God and with our fellows.

"There is no so brilliant war," he declares, "as a war with wrong, no hero so fit to be sung as he who has gained the bloodless victory of truth and mercy."[22]

Love to man and love to God will bring in a better day, "a day of reciprocity and free intimacy between all souls and God. . . . Beauty, truth, and worship, song, science, and duty, will all be unfolded together in this common love."[23]

3. Bushnell was forward looking, one of God's experimenters. Yet he also valued highly the best in the past. His address, "The Age of Homespun,"[24] pays glowing tribute to the sterling qualities and noble customs of the earlier days. His passage on the contribution of the young wife to the success of the new home is noteworthy.[25]

In conclusion, a word should be said about Bushnell's versatility.[26] He was a great preacher, orator, writer, and theologian; he was interested in national and municipal affairs, a promoter of public education and of better social conditions. He invented a furnace, and had skill as an engineer, especially in relation to roads. He was an athlete and enjoyed hiking and fishing. While a student at Yale, he was one of the founders of the Beethoven Society, and he always had the forward-looking anticipation of new truth to be discovered that characterizes the scientist and educator.

And yet he never had any special prominence of position or honor[27] and never did anything spectacular. This is worthy of careful thought by youth today. Perhaps its interpretation is something like this: If one does his own work well, day after day, in his

[21] The same, p. 38.

[22] The same, p. 26.

[23] The same, p. 41.

[24] The same, pp. 368-402.

[25] The same, p. 383.

[26] *Horace Bushnell and Religious Education*, pp. 140-147.

[27] Archibald, Warren Seymour. *Horace Bushnell.* Hartford, E. V. Mitchell, 1930, pp. 147 and 154-155. *Horace Bushnell and Religious Education*, pp. 176-177.

own small sphere, he may make a lasting contribution to human welfare.

Like other brilliant writers and speakers, Bushnell coined many striking phrases and sentences. Two reveal qualities that might well characterize youth today. At first sight they may seem contradictory, but they belong together. However, they must be pondered over to get their full significance. He was "one of God's experimenters" is one. The other is "I fell into the habit of talking with God on every occasion,"—the *habit* of talking with God!

For Discussion

1. Does the forward look, the attitude of anticipating the future and welcoming change, reveal true faith or the lack of faith? Why?
2. In what way can my church relate itself helpfully to civic and national problems? What are some of these crucial issues (housing, parks and playgrounds, schools, labor and capital, foreign policy, etc.)?
3. How does the educational work in my church compare with the best in school, high school, and college? If it can be improved, show where and how in some detail.
4. All will readily admit that parents should create a home with a lovely atmosphere of camaraderie, mutual thoughtfulness, and Christian spirit. What do young people do to promote or to prevent such home life? What can young people do now to prepare themselves for creating such a home of their own?
5. Young people now demand play (or is it entertainment?). Play is necessary if one works. To what degree is the opposite true?
6. For what worthy end are the young people in this church banded together? The young people of the world? What can young people do to make their influence for good a factor in improving human conditions?

For Further Reading

Bushnell, Horace. *Building Eras in Religion.* New York, Scribner, 1881.

————. *Views of Christian Nurture and of Subjects Adjacent Thereto.* Hartford, Edwin Hunt, 1847.

————. *Work and Play, or Literary Varieties.* New York, Scribner, 1871.

Archibald, Warren Seymour. *Horace Bushnell.* Hartford, E. V. Mitchell, 1930.

Cheney, Mary Bushnell. *Life and Letters of Horace Bushnell.* New York, Harper, 1880.

Munger, Theodore T. *Horace Bushnell, Preacher and Theologian.* Boston, Houghton Mifflin, 1899.

Myers, A. J. William. *Horace Bushnell and Religious Education.* Boston, Manthorne & Burack, 1937.

Trumbull, H. Clay. *Litchfield County, Connecticut.* Philadelphia, Sunday School Times Co., 1902.

Warner, Charles Dudley (editor). *Library of the World's Best Literature, Ancient and Modern.* New York, Peale and Hill, 1897, Vol. V.

Martin Luther

by

James V. Thompson[1]
Chairman, Division of Religious Education
Drew University

THE WORLD IN WHICH LUTHER LIVED

During the days when Christopher Columbus was discovering a new world, a frail, nine-year-old child attended the village school in a little Saxon town. Isabella, the Catholic Queen, had given the great admiral her jewels so that he might find new dominions for the Roman Catholic Church and for the glory of her country, Spain. Little did the great Navigator dream that all the territories his discoveries should add would be as nothing compared to the loss the Roman Church would suffer when this frail child, grown into the man, Martin Luther, left it to become the power that should shake that church to its very foundation.

It was a strange new world in which young Martin Luther lived. It was an exciting world, full of tales of strange, new lands. Commerce was growing by leaps and bounds, and a new class of merchants and artisans was rising to demand a share of power equal with that of the hereditary nobility. Currents of new learning were coursing throughout the continent. There was a new interest in literature and in the arts. Men were beginning to exercise a new freedom in their thoughts. Peasants were demanding new rights, a greater degree of justice. Modern nations were in the making. It was the end of the Middle Ages.

The Germany in which Luther lived was not a nation. It was a loosely organized group of states under the leadership of the so-called

[1] The research and assembly of data for this chapter is the work of Mr. Raymond A. Valenzuela, of Drew University, Madison, N. J.

Holy Roman Emperor, a title first used by Charlemagne. The real power was in the hands of the feudal lords and in the governments of the "free cities." Many of these feudal lords were also clergymen, owning allegiance to the Pope at Rome. In a day when nationalistic sentiment was rapidly rising, this allegiance to a power outside Germany was resented.

Living in a day when the church has so little temporal power, it is hard for us to imagine the tremendous power of the Roman Catholic Church of Luther's day. There had been no strong central authority in Germany such as the King of England or the King of France. Consequently, there was no one to curb the great power and abuses of the Church. It has been estimated that the Church, through the Lord Bishops and through the wealthy monasteries, owned more than a third of all Germany. This powerful church became corrupt, and patriotic Germans became eager to destroy the temporal power of the Church over the national life.

It is easy to exaggerate the corruption of the Church, yet at very best it is a picture that is shameful. To understand the resentment the church abuses aroused, helps us to understand the Reformation. The outstanding forms of corruption were those connected with the exploitation of fraudulent relics of saints, with the sale of church offices, and with the sale of certificates of indulgences. Enormous amounts of money came into the church through the exhibition of (supposed) relics, such as the hair or the bones of some great saint. Still greater were the revenues that came through indulgences. These were certificates that were sold for cash, stating that the buyer was released by the Pope from the necessity of doing penance for the indicated misdeeds. How the sale of Church offices and the sale of indulgences—the greatest scandal in the beginning of the sixteenth century—were related to the beginnings of the Reformation is a fascinating story.

At the age of twenty, Albert, Prince of the House of Brandenburg, was already Archbishop of Magdeburg and Bishop of Halberstadt. At the age of twenty-four he was elected to the Archbishopric of Mainz, the highest ecclesiastical position in Germany. To obtain the confirmation of the Pope for his appointment, Albert paid the Holy See 30,000 ducats. This he had borrowed from the Fuggers, the Rothschilds of the sixteenth century. To enable Albert to repay this loan, the Pope granted him a monopoly on the sale of indulgences in several large districts of Germany. Half of the takings were to go to the House of Fuggers and half to the Pope, who was in urgent need of funds for the construction of the $50,000,000 St. Peter's Cathedral in Rome. John Tetzel, the agent, an unscrupulous monk, descended to extremes in his methods of salesmanship. After he had given terrifying descriptions of the horrors of purgatory, he assured the ignorant, superstitious listeners that through the powerful indulgences that he was offering not only they could be saved but even the souls then in purgatory could be released. Tradition has put into his mouth this couplet, "when the coin in the casket rings, the soul to heaven wings."

One man arose to challenge the horrible fraud. Unable to see such things going on in the name of religion, Martin Luther set forth his objections in a series of propositions, which he offered to debate with anyone. As he nailed these "Ninety-Five Theses" to the chapel door at Wittenberg, Luther could not know that he was thus giving the signal for a mighty movement of protest. Had he known, he might not have taken this step, for Luther loved his Church. What kind of person was this man Luther?

YEARS OF GROWTH

Martin Luther, son of Hans Luther and Margarethe Ziegler, was born in the town of Eisleben, in Saxon Germany, on the tenth day of November in 1483. When Martin was six months old, his parents moved to the neighboring town of Mansfeld, where they lived the rest of their days. The early years in Mansfeld were years of privation, but gradually hard work and native resourcefulness triumphed. From being a common laborer, Hans Luther rose to the ownership of furnaces and a position as trusted Councilor of the village.

Martin Luther's early years at home were not very happy ones. Here discipline was rigid, cruel, and unsympathetic. A sensitive lad, he lived in constant fear of punishments. Later in life he said that this fear was responsible for his decision to become a monk. He recognized that his parents "meant it all for the best good," but when he had children of his own he treated them with unusual kindness and sympathy. Remembering his own childhood, he said "the apple ought always to lie beside the rod."

The hours in the village school were no happier. He later referred to the Mansfeld school as "a hell and a purgatory in which children are tortured with cases and tenses, and in which, with much trembling and flogging, they learn nothing." As a man, he used his mighty influence to further the cause of popular education. Three hundred years before Horace Mann, he advocated compulsory, universal, state-supported education. His pleas for attractive schoolrooms, for the inclusion of music and gymnastics in the curriculum, for division of pupils into grade groups sound surprisingly modern when we consider the day in which he lived.

At the age of thirteen, Martin was sent away to school in Magdeburg. The following year he went to Eisenach, where he had relatives. In accordance with the custom of the poorer scholars, he supported himself in school by singing and begging in the streets. Life was made much more pleasant in Eisenach when he was befriended by a wealthy matron, Frau Cotta. The school at Eisenach was very superior, and Luther saw happy days.

Having shown aptitude as a scholar, Martin Luther entered the University of Erfurt at the age of 17. Erfurt was probably the finest university in Germany at the time. Here he took his bachelor's degree in 1502 and the master's degree two and a half years later, concentrating in philosophy and literature.

Hans Luther, prospering now, and able to help him, planned for his son a career as a lawyer. Thus, Martin Luther entered the school of law. In the summer of 1505 he suddenly announced his decision to enter a monastery. His bitterly disappointed father was furious and opposed the move with all his power. Martin's friends, who knew him as a sociable fellow and a lovable person, were shocked beyond measure. But neither the opposition of the father nor the pleas of the friends could move him, and on July 1, 1505, after a rousing farewell party, the monastery doors closed behind him.

What had happened? Luther had been profoundly unhappy. He did not in the least care for law school. Always a sensitive person, he was deeply concerned about the welfare of his soul. The fear of hell was a very real thing to him. In 1505, as a result of his serious illness and the sudden death of a friend, this fear became overwhelming. Returning from his home, he was caught in a terrific thunderstorm. He threw himself on the ground in mortal fear, crying out to the patron saint of miners, "Help, good Saint Anna, I will become a monk."

This decision he hastened to keep.

No monk ever took his duties more seriously. It is probable that he injured his health permanently in the long fasts and lonely vigils. "If ever a monk got to heaven by monkish performances," he tells us, "I should have got there." Yet he found not that peace of soul he so earnestly desired. However, he made progress in the medieval theology. In 1507 he was ordained to the priesthood. Sensing that it would be more healthful for the promising young clergyman to get away from the loneliness of his cell, his wise superior, John Von Staupitz, the vicar of the order, sent him to Wittenberg University. Here he took his degree as a Bachelor of Theology. He was then sent to Erfurt to lecture, in preparation for assuming a full professorship at Wittenberg.

He had risen to a place of respect in the Roman Catholic Augustinian priestly order, and in 1510 he was sent to Rome as a representative. He was deeply disappointed during this pilgrimage to observe the worldliness, even in the highest places of the Church, in Rome, but there is no indication that he rebelled in any way at this time.

Shortly after his return, he resumed his studies in Wittenberg, and in 1512 he became a Doctor of Theology. Immediately thereafter he began a series of lectures on the Bible.

In spite of all his efforts, Luther had thus far failed to find the real peace that he so greatly desired. He had been taught that through the rigid practice of self-discipline he might hope to secure peace with God. Finding no peace in the conditional promises of the Church, his days were lived in anxious fear of the Awful Judge. In his quest for assurance of salvation, Luther studied earnestly the great writings of the Church, the writings of St. Bernard, and of St. Augustine, and of St. Paul. The German mystic, Tauler, gave him the example of the experience of personal relation to God. But it was St. Paul who furnished the key to the peace for which he was searching. He tells us that it suddenly came to him one day that the passages that referred to the "righteousness of God" did not refer to a merciless Judge. As he pondered over the words "The just shall live by faith," he realized that God was not an angry Judge, but one whose righteousness provides forgiveness to them that have faith.

It is not easy to break with the ideas one has held since childhood. It took Luther four more years of hard thinking to understand completely what the new insight meant. So gradual was this change that he did not realize how far he had departed from the current teachings of the Church. By 1517, however, he had come to know, through the joy of his own actual experience, that it is possible so to trust God that one may have the assurance of salvation. He became certain, therefore, that salvation came not through merit due to the works of men, nor the intercession of the Church acting through Pope or priest. Salvation depended wholly upon the forgiving grace of God, to whom the individual person could come, and from whom he could receive the assurance of this forgiveness. This Luther came to call "justification by faith."

LUTHER, THE EMBATTLED REFORMER

Luther was wholly unprepared, however, for the tremendous excitement that his Ninety-Five Theses caused throughout Germany. He had merely posted a series of propositions for purposes of debate, calling attention to some very obvious abuses. He had not, except by implication, attacked the system of indulgences itself, and yet suddenly he found himself a marked figure. German people by thousands had been awaiting the word of a leader to express their feelings.

Luther's protest was not heeded by the Church, and the "upstart monk" was asked to be silent. To defend himself, Luther found that he must either broaden his attack or retreat. To orders and to entreaties that he give up, he replied, "If this be not begun in God's name, it will soon come to naught. But if it be, let Him look after it."

Luther soon found that in attacking the income of the Church he had attacked it in a most sensitive place. He found that he was attacking the whole system of penances and the authority of the Church itself in its relation to the salvation of the individual.

Luther was ordered to retract. This he refused to do. The crisis in the struggle came at Leipzig during a great debate with the able

Dr. John Eck. Eck drove Luther to declare that in many respects he agreed with the opinions of John Huss. Triumphantly he forced from Luther the admission that in condemning Huss, the great council of Constance had made a mistake. Luther had already denied the authority of the Pope. He had now denied the authority of the councils. He made his appeal to the authority of the Word of God—but the Church of Rome had no room for the rebel who denied both the authority of the Pope and that of the Church.

In the summer of 1520 Pope Leo X declared Martin Luther to be a heretic and issued a Bull of Excommunication in which he cast him out of the communion of the Roman Catholic Church.

But Luther refused to be cast out. He protested the injustice of the verdict. In dramatic fashion he proclaimed his defiance, publicly burning the Bull of Excommunication. He was not convinced that with Rome there could be no peace. With a deepening conviction that he was in the right, and that the entire system of salvation by the Church was in the wrong, he took up the battle for his faith with a fierce joy.

In that same year, 1520, Luther attacked his enemies and rallied his friends in three vigorous writings, the address "To the Christian Nobility of the German Nation," the tract on "The Babylonian Captivity of the Church," and "The Essay on Christian Liberty." Luther became one of the most powerful writers the world has seen. The sheer logic of his words as he accused the Church of corruption and malignant error rallied powerful support to his side.

But the Roman church's attempts to discipline Luther had not yet been abandoned. In 1521, Charles V, newly crowned Holy Roman Emperor, summoned the Imperial German Diet to the city of Worms. On April 17, 1521, Luther was called to appear before this Emperor and the assembled German nobles. The Church had already decided that Luther was a heretic. The civil authority must now decide whether or not he should be made to suffer the heretic's death. The representative of the Pope showed Luther a stack of books. Luther admitted that he had written them. Immediately he was asked to repudiate what he had written. Taken by surprise, Luther asked for a time for reflection.

The next day his answer came, clear and strong. He admitted that he had at times expressed himself too violently in his attacks upon various persons. The beliefs that he had expressed, however, he would not retract unless he were convinced that they were contrary to reason and to the Holy Scriptures. Whether or not Luther actually closed with the words, "I cannot do otherwise. Here I stand. God help me. Amen" is not known; nothing, however, could better express the humble determination of the man who knew that God was on his side, though the whole world might be against him.

But Luther was not alone. His sovereign, Frederick the Wise, the Elector of Saxony, and other powerful noblemen rallied to his support. After some of these noblemen had left for home, the Diet passed the "Edict of Worms," in which Martin Luther was condemned to death. The Emperor, however, was never strong enough to enforce the Diet's order, because of the powerful support of the Lutheran noblemen, and thus Luther escaped the fate of John Huss.

On his return from Worms, some friends, fearing for his safety, kidnapped Luther and took him to the impregnable castle of the Wartburg, where he remained in hiding until the immediate danger had passed. Here he found time to translate the New Testament into vernacular German. Later he thus translated the entire Bible.

Meanwhile, his followers in Wittenberg were attempting to break away from all Catholic influence by destroying images and radically changing the forms of worship. Risking his life, Luther returned to Wittenberg and promptly restored order. Until the day of his death, a large part of his energy was devoted to a struggle with those who would overthrow all authority, whether civil or religious, in the name of individual liberty.

Luther was by temperament a great conservative. We have seen how slowly he came to his decisions, and with what reluctance he had left the Roman Catholic Church. It shocked him to see the ease with which others repudiated those things he once held sacred. When he saw the peasants using his doctrines to justify violence and rebellion, he angrily denounced them, and advised the use of harsh measures to subdue them. He has probably been justly criticized for this, but he believed that civil rulers were ordained of God, and thus had no sympathy with revolutionists.

The years from 1521 until his death in 1546 were full of strife and controversy. On the one hand, there was the constant struggle with the power of the Roman Catholic Church and its supporters. These would have uprooted the heresy of the Lutherans even though that might mean war and carnage. On the other hand, Luther had to combat those elements within the new group who differed from Luther in their theological views. These controversies of word and pen often took bitter and violent forms. Thus, Luther's last days were much embittered.

Though the world around him was storm ridden, there was peace in Luther's home. In 1525, Luther married an escaped nun, Catharine Von Bora. She was a woman of great ability and utterly devoted to her husband. She was a splendid mother to his six children, efficiently and economically managed the affairs of a large household, and tenderly cared for Luther during his frequent days of pain and sickness.

In these later years, Luther did an enormous amount of work. He wrote and translated hymns. He translated the Old Testament. He established the form of worship for the Reformed Church and wrote its catechism. He was in constant correspondence with the leaders of the ever-growing Protestant movement. He continued his lectures as a professor in the University and as preacher in the town chapel.

When the end of his life came in 1546, he had seen the Reformation spread over the greater part of Germany into Denmark and Sweden and Norway; and the parallel movements in England and Sweden were well under way.

WHAT THE WORLD OWES MARTIN LUTHER

Sir William Hamilton, writing a nineteenth-century biography of Luther, tells us that he found many descriptions of Luther as angel, quite as many of Luther as devil, but "not a single true portrait of Luther, the man." Patient research has rescued the man, and an intensely human being he is, with serious faults as well as great virtues. No man has shown greater love for children. When his infant daughter Elizabeth died, he wrote to a friend, "My little Elizabeth, my wee daughter is dead. It is wonderful how sorrowful she has left me. My soul is almost like a woman's, so moved am I with misery. I could never have believed that the hearts of parents are so tender towards their children. Pray the Lord for me."

When one comes to judge the value of Luther's permanent contribution, he finds the opinion of the world torn in two. Joseph Clayton, his most recent biographer does not exaggerate. This Roman Catholic writer says:

To this day Martin Luther is praised and his name revered in non-Catholic Christian denominations for having wrought deliverance from the authority of Rome, for bringing the gift of private judgment in faith and morals to all believers. Similarly on the other hand, among Catholics Luther is held in abhorrence as an apostate monk who drew countless souls into heresy and whole nations into schism, the evil of whose life has lived after him.[2]

It is inevitable that we each judge the work of Luther in the light of our own basic convictions. The Catholic is inclined to see nothing but evil, the Protestant nothing but good. Perhaps neither one is wholly right. No sincere Christian can rejoice to see the present disunity of the Church of Christ. For the Catholic, nothing justifies disunity, and thus he willingly submits his private judgment to the authority of the Church.

But, says the Protestant, is it not possible to pay too high a price for unity? Luther did not rebel against unity, he rebelled against a tyranny that denied to the individual the assurance of salvation and a direct relation to God. Schleiermacher has said that the Roman Catholic Church makes the relation of the individual to Christ depend upon his relation to the Church. Protestantism makes the relation of the individual to the Church depend upon his relation to Christ.

Because Luther at Worms stood firm to protect the freedom of intercourse between man and God, and God's witness thereto, the Protestant will always be grateful to him.

The Christian, however, will always strive for the true unity: unity that allows for honest differences of judgment. It is here that we may wish that Luther had been more tolerant in his attitude toward those who differed from him on what, to us, seem minor theological points.

Luther's contributions include the breaking of the power of the

---

[2] Clayton, Joseph. *Luther and His Work.* Milwaukee, Bruce, 1937, p. xxxii.

Roman Church, his influence on German speech, and his aid to the cause of education; but even these do not exhaust his influence.

Although Luther had little sympathy with political democracy, many historians believe that by denying the control of the Church over the State, and by asserting the equal importance of each individual before God, regardless of his calling, he made possible the development of modern political democracy. Especially by his assertion of the right of individual judgment he contributed mightily to this cause. In breaking down the gulf that existed between the clergy and the laity, by stating that every honest occupation was equally pleasing in the sight of God, and by insisting on the immediate social application of salvation, he turned the eyes of the world from some future life to a consideration of the betterment of this world, here and now. This renewed interest in actual living persons now on earth has been of the utmost importance in the development of our modern social order.

Martin Luther—Saint or Devil; Democrat or Dogmatist—what do you say of him?

For Discussion

1. How can a man, tender and generous to children and his own home, be hard, cruel, and violent toward his enemies?
2. Discuss Luther's contribution to political democracy.
3. If Luther's position that we are justified by faith is correct, why do churches insist so strongly upon programs of action? e.g., Youth in Action Program?
4. Compare the effect of Wycliffe's and Luther's translations of the Bible upon the common people of their lands.
5. Why should Protestants and Roman Catholics hold such violently opposite judgments of Martin Luther's life and work?

For Further Reading

Muzzey, David S. "Luther." *Spiritual Heroes.* New York, Doubleday, 1902, p. 268ff.

A brief and fascinating account of the life of Luther and an estimate of his place among the spiritual heroes of mankind. Written before the publication of the findings of modern

Luther scholarship, it is not so complete as the later accounts. It is still, however, one of the finest, shortest accounts we have.

Booth, Edwin P. *Martin Luther, Oak of Saxony.* New York, Round Table Press, 1933.

This is an appreciative and well-written biography. It is rather brief and yet it incorporates most of the discoveries of the modern scholars. It is a well-rounded presentation. One cannot help feeling after reading this book that one has been in contact with a truly great man.

Clayton, Joseph. *Luther and His Work.* Milwaukee, Bruce, 1937.

This biography presents Luther and the days of the Reformation from the point of view of a Catholic. There are excellent historical chapters that are well worth reading. This book shows how divided the opinion of Catholics and of Protestants is concerning the work of Luther.

McGiffert, A. C. *Martin Luther, The Man and His Work.* New York, Appleton-Century, 1911.

Smith, H. Preserved. *The Life and Letters of Martin Luther.* Boston, Houghton Mifflin, 1911.

These two books have been the standard popular biographies of Martin Luther. McGiffert's book gives fine accounts of the boyhood days of Luther and is extremely interesting throughout. There are frequent quotations from Luther's letters. The book by Preserved Smith is very largely made up of Luther's letters. There is probably no better way to come into contact with the vital, vigorous quality of Luther's life than by reading his letters.

Fife, Robert Herndon. *Young Luther.* New York, Macmillan, 1928.

The subtitle of this book is "The Intellectual and Religious Development of Martin Luther to 1518." Here is a fine study of the reasons that led Luther to break with the Roman Catholic Church. Fife says that Luther's religious ideas were "Born at a student's desk no less than at a monk's prayer-stool and were nourished to full stature in a professor's classroom."

Alexander Campbell

by

EVA JEAN WRATHER
Author
Nashville, Tenn.

. . . .

That genius beautiful and great. . . .
With a bit of Andrew Jackson's air,
More of Henry Clay
And the statesmen of Thomas Jefferson's day:
With the face of age,
And the flush of youth,
And that air of going on, forever free. . . .

And oh the music of each living throbbing thing
When Campbell arose
A pillar of fire,
The great high priest of the Spring.

He stepped from out the Brush Run Meetinghouse
To make the big woods his cathedrals,
The river his baptismal font,
The rolling clouds his bells. . . .
Richer grew the rushing blood
Within our fathers' coldest thought.
Imagination at the flood
Made flowery all they heard.
The deep communion cup
Of the whole South lifted up. . . .

The heroes of faith from the days of Abraham
Stood on that blue-grass ground—

While the battle-ax of thought
Hewed to the bone
That the utmost generation
Till the world was set right
Might have an America their own. . . .

He preached with faultless logic
An American Millennium:
The social order
Of a realist and farmer
With every neighbor
Within stone wall and border.
And the tongues of flame came down
Almost in spite of him. . . .[1]

I

On September 12, 1788, a son, whom they named Alexander, was born to Jane and Thomas Campbell, of County Antrim, North Ireland. Jane Corneigle Campbell was of French descent, and she was fully imbued with the independent spirit of her Huguenot ancestors who, for the sake of liberty of conscience, had fled France after the revocation of the Edict of Nantes in 1685 to set up their homes and their pulpits in a strange land. Thomas Campbell, a Scotsman of Clan Argyle, whose people had lived in Ireland since the Plantation of Ulster, was also of resolute temper. His father, Archibald Campbell, a crusty old soldier who had seen service under General Wolfe at the Battle of Quebec, had forsworn Roman Catholicism for the faith of the Church of England and demanded that his four sons likewise should "serve God according to act of Parliament."[2] But conscience, not an act of Parliament, would always decide Thomas Campbell in his course. As it was in the simple, austere meeting-houses of the Presbyterians that he found his God, Thomas, in spite of all protest from his father, had determined to enter the Presbyterian ministry, and he held to his resolution so firmly that Archibald finally relented and sent him away to Scot-

[1] Lindsay, Vachel. "Alexander Campbell." *Collected Poems.* New York, Macmillan, 1925.

[2] Richardson, Robert. *Memoirs of Alexander Campbell.* Philadelphia, Lippincott, 1868, vol. I, p. 24.

land to study. Naught in worldly wealth, but a goodly heritage of character, would Jane and Thomas Campbell bequeath to their children.

An independent and resolute spirit would serve a lad well who was born in the year 1788, for it was an age suffused in an atmosphere of new hopes and new enterprises. Across the Atlantic to the west, a few scattered colonies had waged successfully a war to free themselves from the yoke of Britain, and across the channel to the east, in France, another revolution was brewing. The Industrial Revolution and unprecedented progress in scientific discovery and invention was opening a new world to man's ken and calling into question much that he had taken for granted in his old world. A child of his age, young Alexander Campbell of County Antrim was not of a temper to fear the new because it was new or to hold to the past when a tradition had become outworn.

When Alexander was ten years old, his father Thomas, having finished an eight years' course of study at the University of Glasgow and at a theological seminary, and having served a term as probationer, was given his first pastorate—the little church of Ahorey, near the village of Richhill in County Armagh—and he moved his family to a farm in the new pastorate. Still all was not well with Jane and Thomas Campbell. Their firstborn, though he had spent several years in his uncles' academy in the city of Newry, was showing little progress in his studies, while with the greatest zeal he would occupy the day hunting rabbits or fishing in the waters of Lough Neagh. Finally, they hit upon a plan. They took Alexander away from school and put him to work on the farm, thinking thus, said Thomas, "to break him in to his books." The plan was a success. After a year or two of work on the land, pleasant though it was, Alexander announced to his parents his intention of becoming "one of the best scholars in the kingdom."[3]

Thomas Campbell gladly undertook the office of tutor to his son, and Alexander began the study of literature, philosophy, French, and, of course, in preparation for the university, Latin and Greek. Especially thorough was his reading of John Locke's *Essay on the Human Understanding*. There, in Locke's empirical psychology

[3] *Memoirs of Alexander Campbell*, vol. I, p. 32.

bound by observation and freed from supernatural assumptions, a young thinker began to find his method. The concepts in this system of the devout English philosopher which in the hands of others had led to materialism and skepticism were counterbalanced in Alexander's thought by his own innate awareness of "the mystery of Godliness" and by his coming under the influence, a few years later, of the Scottish School of Philosophy—Thomas Reid's School of Common Sense—which had done a good service by drawing a clear distinction between the realm of the senses and the realm of the spirit, between the function of science and the function of religion. Also with great eagerness, young Alexander read Locke's *Letters Concerning Toleration,* and, in the midst of oppressed and strife-ridden Ireland, wings were given to his ideals of civil and religious liberty. After some years, Thomas Campbell, to augment his meager income, moved his family into Richhill and opened an academy. Alexander, at sixteen, was sufficiently advanced in his studies to become his father's assistant.

In 1807, Thomas Campbell's health failed, and he was ordered to take a voyage to America. Alexander, who, at eighteen, was now head of the family, continued to run his father's academy and also acted as tutor to the children of the lord of Richhill manor. Thomas Campbell liked the new country across the Atlantic so well that in the following year he wrote his family to join him. In the fall of 1808, Alexander, his mother, and six younger brothers and sisters set sail from Londonderry.

But fate was to give a queer twist to their fortunes. Their ship very soon ran into a heavy storm and was wrecked off the coast of Islay, one of the islands of the Hebrides. In the midst of the storm, Alexander, who had had some thoughts of a literary career, calmly considered the vanities of the world and dedicated himself to the ministry. All the passengers were saved from the shipwreck; but the Campbells, not desiring to begin another voyage at so stormy a season, decided to spend the winter in Scotland, where Alexander might turn bad fortune into good by realizing his ambition of following in his father's footsteps to the University of Glasgow. With the zeal of one who knew he must crowd all his formal college training into one short year, Alexander threw himself into his work. At four in the morning he arose to study—logic, belles lettres, Latin,

Greek, French, and experimental philosophy, accompanied by experiments in natural science, were the classes he elected—and he stayed at his books until ten at night. He finished his course as an honor student, winning a coveted prize in logic.

On July 31, 1809, the Campbells again set sail for America. Fifty-one days later they first sighted New York. As Thomas Campbell, on his arrival in America two years before, had immediately been assigned to the Presbytery of Chartiers in western Pennsylvania, his family now made their way to Philadelphia and thence by the famed Old Glade Road, over which Washington had once led his troops, to the little frontier village of Washington, Pennsylvania. Happily reunited with Thomas, they were surprised at the story of his experiences.

II

Thomas Campbell had begun his ministry in a communion which, if completely described, would be called the Old Light Anti-Burgher Secession Presbyterian Church, and every name in the title represented a bitter schism in the mother Church of Scotland. Irenic and tolerant, Thomas was sorely distressed by the division and bickering that he felt were making a mockery of the religion Christ had died to establish. While pastor of Ahorey, he had tried, unsuccessfully, to get the various branches of Presbyterianism to unite, having carried the case in 1806 directly before the General Associate Synod of Scotland. He had also joined a liberal interdenominational organization for the propagation of the gospel, called the Evangelical Society, but the Associate Synod of Ireland had demanded that he take no active part in its work.

On coming to the new world, he had, to his disappointment, found that sectarianism had merely changed its climate and not its character in crossing the Atlantic. Preachers were few on the frontier, and Thomas Campbell had soon learned that many Christians went for years without the solace of the Lord's Supper because no clergyman of their particular party was present to administer the sacrament. The inclusiveness of his Christian love rebelling at this restriction, he had invited his brethren to forget their differences and remembering only their common faith in the Christ to join in the communion of the Lord's Supper. The Presbytery of

Chartiers, astounded at this heterodoxy, had severely rebuked him. The Associate Synod of North America also had made its displeasure known.

Finally, Thomas Campbell, despairing of an understanding, had renounced the authority of the Presbytery and Synod and continued his preaching as an independent minister. Most of his parishioners were, like himself, Scots-Irish immigrants and, remaining loyal to their pastor, they had joined him in forming the Christian Association of Washington, a non-sectarian society for the purpose of advocating his plea for Christian unity and liberality. Defining his intent in the slogan, "Where the Scriptures speak, we speak; where the Scriptures are silent, we are silent,"[4] Thomas Campbell had immediately occupied himself with writing a *Declaration and Address* to set forth the ideals of the Association. The document had gone to press while his family were sailing toward the harbor of New York. Thus matters stood when the Campbells were reunited in Washington, Pennsylvania.

Alexander was pleased and relieved at the turn of events, for, having come under the influence of a liberal independent minister while in Glasgow, and having conscientiously and critically attended the services of every denomination in the large city, he had come to feel cramped within the confines of his old faith—"I imbibed disgust at the popular schemes chiefly while a student at Glasgow,"[5] he later wrote—and he had privately renounced his allegiance to the Seceder Presbyterians. Now he found his resolve was in agreement with his father's, and eagerly he read the *Declaration and Address* as soon as the proof sheets came from the press.

This fifty-four-page document was a plea for the "unity, peace, and purity" of the Church, many parts of which sounded as if they might have been lifted from Locke's *Letters Concerning Toleration*. "Tired and sick of the bitter jarrings and janglings of a party spirit," it declared, "we would desire to be at rest." This ideal of "a permanent scriptural unity among Christians" was to be attained "by removing the stumbling-blocks—the rubbish of ages"—all those complex dogmas that had gradually evolved to divide Christendom into warring camps—and thus to "come fairly and firmly to original

[4] *Memoirs of Alexander Campbell*, vol. I, p. 236.

[5] The same, p. 176.

ground . . . and take up things just as the apostles left them." Religion, reasoned the document, should demand agreement on only a few "fundamental truths," a few "first principles," while in all other matters, in all interpretations of metaphysical questions, each man should be left free to form and hold his own opinion—"every man must be allowed to judge for himself, as every man must bear his own judgment." The United States, "a country happily exempted from the baneful influence of a civil establishment of any peculiar form of Christianity," was exalted as the ideal place for the commencement of such a movement for Christian unity.[6] Free and democratic citizens of the new Republic should be the precursors of a free and democratic Church.

To Alexander Campbell it seemed that his father had written America's religious Declaration of Independence. Solemnly he pledged his future to the support of its ideals. Realistically perceiving that the plea might not be so simple as it sounded on the surface, he made a rigid schedule of study to prepare himself for his work. Church history and theology were added to the list of his former studies, and he began to acquire a mastery of Hebrew, in order that he could know the Bible in its original tongues. In 1811, the Christian Association, unable to attract others to its Christian unity movement, reluctantly resolved itself into an independent church, erecting a meeting-house near Brush Run; one of its first acts was to license Alexander Campbell, age twenty-two, to preach the gospel. The following year he was ordained.

The year 1811 brought another important change in his life. He married Margaret Brown, only daughter of a prosperous farmer, and moved to her home in western Virginia.[7] A few years later he became a man of property when his father-in-law deeded to him the farm and comfortable house on Buffaloe Creek. In 1812, his first child was born, and a religious issue was precipitated. Should the baby be baptized?

Alexander Campbell, even as Thomas, wished to espouse a broad plan for Christian union, but he was convinced that the two sacra-

[6] *Memoirs of Alexander Campbell*, vol. I, pp. 242-244, 252-272. Also Hanna, William Herbert. *Thomas Campbell, Seceder and Christian Union Advocate.* Cincinnati, Standard Publishing Company, 1935, pp. 118-124.

[7] Now in the state of West Virginia.

ments (or ordinances, as he preferred to call them) instituted by the Christ were not questions on which it was permitted man to exercise his own judgment. They were positive precepts to be obeyed, and hence the intelligent Christian must seek correctly to understand their true import and design. From the beginning, the Christian Association had made the weekly observance of the Lord's Supper the very center of adoration in their worship, deeming it was thus with the Apostolic Church. Now Alexander turned to a study of the sacrament of Baptism. Long hours he burned the midnight oil, until finally, he related, he felt himself lifted to "a new peak of the mountain of God."[8] Here he beheld Baptism as a divinely appointed rite signifying the death, burial, and resurrection of the Savior, which to every believer should symbolize his own death in sin, burial in Christ, and resurrection, with sins remitted, to walk in newness of life. Obviously, immersion was the only adequate physical representation of this mystery. Also, he perceived that the following of the Christ must be by *personal* allegiance and, hence, by *free choice;* therefore, Infant Baptism was a development out of harmony with a fundamental principle of the Christian religion. Baby Jane Caroline was not baptized, and her father embraced the doctrine of "Believers' Immersion."

Thomas Campbell, after a brief struggle, surrendered to Alexander's interpretation of the rite of Baptism, and with this acquiescence the leadership of the movement he had initiated passed to his son. It was an inevitable consequence. Thomas, though resolute where a matter of conscience was concerned, was retiring, contemplative, and peace-loving; he could formulate a program, but he could not, through controversy, urge that program upon others. Alexander, on the contrary, was a proud, fiery, self-willed man of action. Not content to hold his beliefs passively, he must try to persuade others to see the truth as he saw it. "I like the bold Christian hero,"[9] he declared, and proved it by his own actions.

But, for a few years, his life passed in obscurity. After the practice of Immersion was adopted, the Brush Run Church was invited to join a Baptist Association. Not wishing to have its plea for Chris-

[8] *Millennial Harbinger,* June, 1848 (series III, vol. V, no. 6), p. 345. A monthly magazine edited and published by Alexander Campbell, Bethany, Virginia, 1830-1864.
[9] *Memoirs of Alexander Campbell,* vol. I, p. 354.

tian unity end in the founding of another denomination, it gladly accepted, and Alexander Campbell contented himself with farming and with preaching to a few Baptist churches in the vicinity.

III

In 1820 came a change. A Presbyterian minister challenged the Baptists to a debate, and the Baptists insisted that Alexander Campbell be their champion. The debate was published, and for the first time Campbell realized the power of the press to disseminate ideas. He set up a printing establishment on his own farm, and in 1823 issued the first number of his magazine, ***The Christian Baptist.***

Seeking to clear the way for his constructive program, he began a slashing attack on everything he considered an abuse in the old systems. From his Huguenot ancestors Alexander Campbell had inherited a full share of the French genius for satire, and with the biting pen of a Voltaire he attacked the tyranny of ecclesiasticism and the dominance of the priesthood, which were fettering men's minds and keeping them from their true birthright in the Kingdom of God. He assaulted the conflicting and complex dogmas that were blinding men's eyes to the beautiful simplicity of the Christian faith. He scoffed at the popular conceptions of the operation of the Holy Spirit in conversion, which denied man all free will and left him helpless to do anything to work his own salvation. He ridiculed the popular literalistic mode of "text-preaching" that considered every sentence in the Bible of equal importance; he offered instead a concept of progressive revelation with a sharp division drawn between the authority of the Old and the New Testaments, and, foreshadowing the work of higher criticism, he made a distinction between the historical portions of the Bible and those parts which were Divinely revealed. He decried the slavish acceptance of creeds, which embalmed belief in static uniformity; and—while insisting that the dogma of private judgment, the thought of the individual, must be disciplined by submission to the qualified opinion of the Church, or, rather, to the consensus of the intelligent opinion of the brotherhood—he demanded that this common mind of the Church, this common reason of the people as a whole, should be left free to develop with the changing centuries.

The aggressive tone of the new journal recommended it to the hardy pioneers of the frontier who took their religion as they did their Indian-fighting—seriously and with vigor. Its exalting of the free will and dignity of man recommended it to the independent empire-builders of a new continent who would make their own peace with God as they wrested their own destinies from the wilderness. The simplicity of its common-sense message and its plea for unity recommended it to all those who were sick of the endless and bitter jangling over questions of abstruse metaphysics. Indeed, the "men of the Western Waters" were quick to realize that the philosophical tools being wielded by the theologian on the Buffaloe were the same as those that had served the Founding Fathers of their republic and that his sane, reasonable, energetic, and adventurous temper was well adapted to the pioneering, scientific, experimental spirit of their age and country. Had not Thomas Jefferson also drawn his inspiration from the writings of John Locke? And did not the little magazine published in the Virginia hills follow the lead of Locke's *Essay on the Human Understanding,* his *Letters Concerning Toleration,* and his *Reasonableness of Christianity* in protesting against scholastic and speculative systems of philosophy and theology; in eschewing emotionalism and declaring that the truths of revelation, like the truths of science, must justify themselves to experience and observation and reason; in denouncing dogmatism and appealing to tolerance and to practical religion and morality; in maintaining that the essentials of the New Testament teaching were few and simple and that its one truth of central import was the Messiahship of Jesus and, hence, that assent to this proposition was sufficient evidence of saving faith?[10] Campbell's became a potent voice in the West. Likewise in the East, denominational publications became aware of a new force entering American religious life—and not for the better, many of them thought.

The Baptists gradually began to agree. Campbellism was declared anathema, and its adherents were successively read out of the Baptist churches. Forced into a separate existence and generally taking the name Disciples of Christ,[11] Campbell and his followers

[10] See *The Disciples of Christ,* a pamphlet, by Edward Scribner Ames, Dean of the Disciples Divinity House, University of Chicago.

[11] This body is also known both as the Christian Church and as the Church of Christ.

insisted they were not just another Christian sect but were, rather, a movement whose chief aim still was to restore the original unity and purity of the Church. There were defects in their vision, and at times they might falter and seem to lose sight of their goal; at times Campbell's logical mind might seem too preoccupied with an authoritative system. But in a period of rabid sectarianism, they had made a beginning toward Christian federation, toward achieving the ideal of "One Holy, Catholic, and Apostolic Church."

In 1830, Campbell, now forty-one years old, discontinued his first publication and started *The Millennial Harbinger,* a monthly magazine that he was to edit for the next thirty-four years and that carried his constructive program for reform. Though at some points his theology was unique, Campbell was well aware that there was nothing startlingly new in this program. While he was still a youth in Ireland, there had been men in the New World seeking to break the shackles of Old World traditions and establish a free Church for a free people. James O'Kelley, a North Carolina Methodist, Abner Jones, a Vermont Baptist, and Barton Stone, a Kentucky Presbyterian, each had started an independent movement; and the three had finally merged, in many parts of the country, into the Christian Connection. Campbell met Barton Stone and was impressed by his passion for Christian union. Their followers, realizing their similarity of aim, began to commune together until almost everywhere throughout the West the bodies became one.

Campbell was pleased with this practical demonstration of unity, but he held some mental reservations toward his new brethren. Stone was a product of the frontier, and his movement was born during the revival fervor of the 1800's. No man could love America and its political ideals more than Alexander Campbell—only a few years after coming to the United States he had written his uncle in Ireland, "I would not exchange the honor and privilege of being an American citizen for the position of your king"[12]—but his was no uncritical allegiance. He was not a product of the frontier; he was a gentleman educated according to the standards of the Old World, and he felt that the emotional phenomena accompanying American revivalism were not an indication of the

[12] *Memoirs of Alexander Campbell,* vol. I, p. 466.

operation of the Holy Spirit, but, rather, were evidence of a false and baleful mysticism founded in hysteria and superstition. He would extricate Christian conversion from obscurantism and quasi-magic and untenable doctrines of providence and grace, and anchor it firmly in objective reality—in a belief on God as He had revealed Himself in history in the Person of the Christ. He would appeal from individual emotion to universal reason and to moralism and action.

This position was evidence of the fundamental difference in the two men: Barton W. Stone was a thoroughgoing Protestant, whereas Alexander Campbell frankly maintained that on some points the Protestant Reformers had run so fast out of Rome that they had run past Jerusalem. Alexander, as a youth, may have listened to his grandfather, Archibald Campbell, expound his High Church concepts. At any rate, like the Catholics, he held that the Church was meant to be constitutionally as well as spiritually one; that schism was sin. He rejected the Protestant compromise of "invisible unity" and insisted on visible, corporate unity and on the "high" doctrine of the Church as the Body of Christ and the instrument by which He now performs His will—even while he retained the Protestant emphasis on the priesthood of all believers, as opposed to sacerdotal claims; on the New Testament as a sufficient witness to the faith and order of the Church; on love and freedom, as opposed to legal discipline and regimentation; and on a personal faith based on trust in and loyalty to the Christ, as opposed to intellectualized forms of belief.[13] To most effectively carry out the work of the Kingdom and to preserve unbroken the concept of the "One Body," Christian union, he felt, must be maintained by visible bonds; but, to safeguard liberty and to assure the free development of thought within the Church for all the ages, those bonds must be as few as possible.

Also like the Catholics, Campbell realized the dramatic value and the deep mystic import of the Christian sacraments. The

[13] Address by William Robinson, Principal of Overdale Theological College, Birmingham, England. *The Christian Advocate* (organ of the Disciples in Great Britain and Ireland, where the communion is uniformly known as the Churches of Christ), August 9, 1935, p. 527.

"low" view that the sacraments were mere commands to be attended to, that the Eucharist was no more than a memorial service, was repugnant to his deepest religious feeling. For Campbell's insistence on Baptism by Believers' Immersion and on the constant weekly observance of the Holy Communion was not founded in any narrow legalism or literalism; it was the outgrowth of his own gradual perception of the philosophical and psychological importance of these sacred ordinances. Man, he believed, not being entirely a creature of the spirit, needs some concrete, some sensual form in which to express his religious devotion; and hence, God in His wisdom had instituted the sacraments, which unite man's emotion, his intellect, and his will—the faculties of "the whole man"—in one sublime act of consecration. Baptism and the Lord's Supper were "the Church's first centre of unity," and they would ever remain, in Campbell's opinion, the two visible symbols of the disciples' unity of faith. The central doctrine of Christianity, the Incarnation, was carried forward in principle in the Church and its sacraments, and considering that dogma was best enshrined in dramatic form, Campbell was impressed with the power of Baptism and the Eucharist to present in simple symbolism the drama of the Cross and the Resurrection. Also, these two rites were social ceremonies, expressive of the *koinonia,* the fellowship, of the passionate love of man at the heart of His teaching; in the fellowship of the Lord's Supper was most beautifully symbolized the *social* import of Christianity, which Campbell liked so well to emphasize. Through the Holy Communion, the worshipers had communion with one another and with the whole Church Universal. Furthermore, here they also held communion with Him. For Campbell did not hesitate to embrace the Catholic doctrine of the sacraments as channels of grace. In partaking of the Lord's Supper, he believed, the worshiper receives a direct renewal of spiritual energy. Campbell scorned the theory of Transubstantiation; yet he did not doubt that to those who receive worthily there is a Real Presence in the holy symbols of the Bread and the Wine. In his ethico-sacramentalism, the miracle was not physical—but spiritual. The sacraments were the Divinely appointed means by which man reaches mystic union with God—a more important thing, after all, he felt, than union with men.[14] Thus, rationalistic French and mystical Celt met in Campbell's concept of faith as the *principle* and the sacraments as the *means* of enjoyment of the grace of God.[15]

Viewed as a whole, then, Campbell's religious system was neither Protestant nor Catholic in the accepted meaning of the terms, and in a sense it formed a *via media* between the two. And did it not suggest a common ground on which they some day might come together? Certainly, Campbell's contemporaries were quite aware of the inclusive nature of his theology. His opponents charged him, at one and the same time, with leaning toward the two extremes of Roman Catholicism and of Unitarianism. Though he radically differed at points from each of these extremes of doctrine, Campbell knew that there were elements of truth in both charges. As he insisted on the validity of a "high" concept of the nature of the Church and the sacraments, characterizing Catholicism, so he embraced certain liberal ideas (latitudinarian, his opponents called them) closely akin to some of the Unitarian principles being advocated in the East by William Ellery Channing. For with a consuming passion for liberty, both religious and civil, Alexander Campbell joined a spirit of devout obedience to the will of God. "I call no man master upon the earth,"[16] he wrote, but he bowed unquestioningly before any precept he conceived to be a commandment of the Christ. Hence, the theology he professed was a compound of liberty and authority—of vital elements in both Protestantism and Catholicism—for of such, Campbell believed, was true Apostolic Christianity.

IV

Many there were who agreed enthusiastically with these precepts.

---

[14] See William Robinson's *Essays on Christian Unity* (London, James Clark)—a study of the problems of the faith, ministry, and sacraments of the Church in relation to the present-day movement toward Christian unity.

[15] Campbell, Alexander. *The Christian System, in Reference to the Union of Christians, and a Restoration of Primitive Christianity, as Plead in the Current Reformation.* Cincinnati, Bosworth, Chose & Hall, 1871 (published by Campbell, Bethany, Va., 1839, a revision of a work first issued in 1835—Campbell's works number more than fifty volumes), p. 174.

[16] *Christian Baptist,* April, 1826 (vol. III, no. 9), p. 353. A monthly magazine edited and published by Alexander Campbell, Bethany, Virginia, from August, 1823, to August, 1830.

Many there were who disagreed violently. In fact, in the earlier years, it was difficult to tell whether Campbell was more loved or more hated, more revered or more feared. To his followers, he was the greatest interpreter of the will of God since the days of the Apostles. To his opponents, he was "the greatest Heresiarch in the Mississippi Valley." But whatever the judgment, it was expressed in superlatives. For Campbell was a man about whom no one ever felt indifferent. Debate might prevail concerning his excellencies or his deficiencies as a theologian, writer, or scholar; but there was no question of Alexander Campbell's easy mastery over an audience, of his possession of that indefinable magnetic quality, that dynamic vitality, and that calm assurance which—from the days of his youth when his face portrayed a fine and ardent idealism until the days of his maturity when he had championed his ideals in so many a hard fight that his features had become those of a rugged warrior, of a veritable roaring Lion of God—marked him as a man born to command.

Tall, erect, heavy dark hair crowning a finely formed head, piercing blue eyes, a high-bridged Roman nose, firmly set lips, and a chin that bespoke determination, Campbell appeared the statesman rather than the minister. In speaking—his diction was clear and rapid and never lost a trace of the burr that so well became the name of Campbell—he scorned all tricks of histrionics or emotionalism and spoke directly and simply, depending for emphasis on his own passionate sincerity and belief in the power of his message. But, even aside from Campbell's impelling personality, his speeches had a dramatic quality all their own. With a mind that renounced all narrow legalism and rejoiced in broad concepts, he would carry his audience on sweeping, extensive views of man, nature, and God; he was a master of the rounded, sonorous periods that marked the highest oratorical eloquence of his generation.

Campbell's was an age in which the debating platform was one of the chief mediums of entertainment and enlightenment, and his ready wit and gift of fluent, extemporaneous speech gained him the reputation of a champion who roamed the countryside seeking whom he might challenge. In truth, Campbell debated far less than most men of his day who were in positions of prominence. He held only five public debates. Only three of these, with Presbyterian ministers, were for the purpose of urging his particular reformatory views. The fourth, with the Roman Catholic Bishop Purcell, defended the Church against those concepts of Christianity which he deemed were Roman and not truly Catholic. The fifth, with the socialist, Robert Owen, ignoring all fleeting problems of form and creed, dealt with the timeless issues of the very bases of man's religious faith. Owen contended for an atheistic co-operative system of society, which lit the beacon for future generations of Communists who would become intent on rendering unto Caesar all the things that are God's. Campbell, in rebuttal, offered a rational *via media* for harmonizing the demands of personal righteousness and of social responsibility to all men who should be concerned about rightly dividing the things that are Caesar's from the things that are God's.

With the passing of the years, as Campbell's radicalism softened into liberalism and his activities took a broader scope, he ceased to be a suspected heretic in the eyes of most of his contemporaries and became the respected leader of one of his country's major bodies of Christians, a body that had the added distinction of being one of America's few indigenous religious movements. Traveling thousands of miles annually, he gradually found the church doors of almost every denomination opened to him. He was invited to address the joint Houses of Congress, and on another visit to Washington was the guest of President Buchanan at the White House. So many thousands of books issued every year from his printing press that the government established a post office on his farm, which he named Bethany, and he held the office of postmaster for thirty years.

Campbell's views and writings gradually spread to Europe, and a *British Millennial Harbinger* was published. In 1847, he made a lecture tour of Great Britain. Carrying a letter of introduction from Henry Clay, he was received in London by the American ambassador and invited to attend a reception at the embassy, where "a noble lady, an intimate and favorite with the Queen," informed him that his book, *Conversations at the Carlton House,* was read in Queen Victoria's household.[17]

[17] "Letters from Europe," No. XI, *Millennial Harbinger,* October, 1847 (series III, vol. IV, no. 10), p. 580.

V

So versatile were Campbell's talents and interests that not even his duties as editor and writer, preacher and debater, could occupy all his attention. Fortunately for the movement that he launched, in Campbell's veins flowed the blood of canny Scots and thrifty French. With a constantly growing family, he never abandoned his early resolve not to accept pay for preaching; and though his press paid dividends in later years, in the beginning he was hard hit to keep it running. Hence, to support his family without neglecting the propagation of his religious views or his obligations of charity, Campbell's business acumen stood him in good stead. He stocked his highland farm with long-wooled sheep and paid such careful attention to the good management of his estate that it gradually increased from three hundred acres and a small house to several thousand acres and a rambling mansion of twenty-five rooms. Over this estate, in his rôle as an affable Virginia country gentleman famed for his hospitality and conversation, Campbell ruled with a genial pride and a high good humor that charmed and sometimes surprised the constant succession of guests who made their way to Bethany from every state in the Union and even from Europe. Campbell's was a philosophy of happiness, and gloom had no place in either his religion or his temperament.

In 1840, he began a new activity. Deeming education the handmaiden of intelligent worship of God and of intelligent citizenship in the republic, he established Bethany College, whose buildings crown the top of a beautiful hill on his farm about a mile from his house. For almost a quarter of a century he served as its president and as a professor holding the chairs of Sacred History, Intellectual Philosophy, Evidences of Christianity, Moral Science, and Political Economy. Exercising his interest in education on a larger field, he was a pioneer in the fight to establish a free school system. As he sought to democratize the Church, so he sought to democratize elementary education.

Nor did even these activities satisfy the high sense of responsibility he felt as a citizen of his adopted country. He was elected a delegate to the Virginia Constitutional Convention of 1829, and the speeches he made before that body contain a penetrating analysis of the attitude of the democratic "men of the Western Waters" toward the more aristocratic and conservative East. Momentous issues were before the state in 1829, and Virginia had sent only her most distinguished sons to chart the course of her revised constitution. During his three months in Richmond, Campbell made the acquaintance of James Madison, matched wits with John Randolph of Roanoke, and sat on a committee with John Marshall.

Though this was his only formal venture into politics, Campbell never slackened his interest in whatever issues affected the welfare of his country. Paramount among these issues was the question of slavery. An eighteenth-century rationalist, fundamentally incapable of fanaticism, Campbell condemned slavery but demanded justice for the slave-owner. "I have always been anti-slavery, but never an abolitionist," he declared. The Bible taught the brotherhood of man, and he would both practice and defend this ideal; but he considered it poor logic and loose thinking to argue that "the brotherhood of man" and "the equality of man" were synonymous or interchangeable terms. Furthermore, the "professional abolitionists," reckless of all social or economic consequences, were openly advocating violence to secure an immediate political end; Campbell was convinced, as he said, that "Christians can never be reformers in any system which uses violence, recommends or expects it." In pungent essay after essay, he pleaded that the extremists on both sides yield the field to the rational anti-slavery men both North and South who were seeking a solution to the complex problem whereby the slaves might be freed without bringing economic and social disaster on the whole South, black and white alike; with an almost clairvoyant look into the future, he warned of the bloodshed and tragedy that were certain to ensue if Christians did not realize their high social responsibility and urge on their fellow citizens this sane middle ground of peace and of justice.[18] Had the counsel of men like Campbell prevailed, there might have been no occasion for war.

When the War Between the States did come, it mercifully found Campbell's mind oblivious to much that transpired around him.

[18] "Our Position to American Slavery," *Millennial Harbinger*, 1845 (series III, vol. II); "The Fugitive Slave Law," 1851 (series IV, vol. I).

Having passed threescore and ten, he was already journeying to lands afar. The intervals when he was aware of current events found him torn between two loyalties—his love of the South and his allegiance to the Union. But of one thing he could well be proud: when other major communions were splitting into two bitter camps, North and South, the Disciples withstood propaganda and war to remain a united body.

Alexander Campbell died on March 4, 1866. At last his soul had broken its earthly shackles and was released into the realm of perfect freedom. For Campbell believed with the Apostle Paul that the Spirit of God is the Spirit of Liberty.

For Further Reading

BIOGRAPHIES OF ALEXANDER CAMPBELL

Grafton, Thomas W. *Alexander Campbell: Leader of the Great Reformation of the Nineteenth Century.* St. Louis, Christian Publishing Company, 1897.

Hudson, John Allen. *The Man and the Moment: A Study in the Life of Alexander Campbell.* Cincinnati, Christian Leader Corporation, 1927.

Richardson, Robert. *Memoirs of Alexander Campbell.* Philadelphia, Lippincott, 1868 and 1870. 2 vols. Reprinted in one volume by Standard Publishing Company, Cincinnati.

Smith, Benjamin Lyon. *Alexander Campbell.* St. Louis, Bethany Press, 1930.

RELIGIOUS CONDITIONS ON THE AMERICAN FRONTIER

Mode, Peter G. *The Frontier Spirit in American Christianity.* New York, Macmillan, 1923.

THE GREAT REVIVAL OF THE 1800'S ON THE FRONTIER, THE "SECOND AWAKENING"

Compare with the "Great Awakening" under Jonathan Edwards in New England.

Cleveland, Catherine C. *The Great Revival in the West, 1797-1805.* Chicago, University of Chicago, 1916.

Rogers, James R. *The Cane Ridge Meeting-house.* Cincinnati, Standard Publishing Company, 1910.

HISTORY OF MOVEMENTS TO FORM A LIBERAL DEMOCRATIC CHURCH PREVIOUS TO CAMPBELL

Morill, Milo True. *A History of the Christian Denomination in America, 1794-1911 A. D.* Dayton, Christian Publishing Association, 1912.

Ware, Charles Crossfield. *Barton Warren Stone: Pathfinder of Christian Union, A Story of His Life and Times.* St. Louis, Bethany Press, 1932.

GENERAL HISTORY OF THE BACKGROUND, ORIGIN, AND PLEA OF THE DISCIPLES OF CHRIST

Garrison, Winfred Ernest. *Religion Follows the Frontier: A History of the Disciples of Christ.* New York, Harper, 1931.

Robinson, William. *What Churches of Christ Stand For.* Birmingham (England), Churches of Christ Publishing Committee, 1926.

BACKGROUND OF ALEXANDER CAMPBELL'S THOUGHT, THEOLOGICAL AND PHILOSOPHICAL

Athearn, Clarence R. *The Religious Education of Alexander Campbell: Morning Star of the Coming Reformation.* St. Louis, Bethany Press, 1928.

Garrison, Winfred Ernest. *Alexander Campbell's Theology: Its Sources and Historical Setting.* St. Louis, Christian Publishing Company, 1900.

BIOGRAPHIES OF DISCIPLE LEADERS CONTEMPORARY WITH CAMPBELL

Baxter, William, *Life of Elder Walter Scott.* St. Louis, Bethany Press, 1926.

Power, Fredrick D. *Life of William Kimbrough Pendleton, LL.D.* St. Louis, Christian Publishing Company, 1902.

Williams, John Augustus. *Life of Elder John Smith.* Cincinnati, Standard Publishing Company, 1904.

Ignatius Loyola

by

LAURA H. WILD
Emeritus Professor of Biblical Literature
Mt. Holyoke College

THE SOCIETY OF JESUS

THE Jesuits, or the Society of Jesus, have been a strong Roman Catholic order ever since Ignatius Loyola, a Spanish soldier, felt the urge for founding such an order. It was the strongest force to combat Luther's idea in starting the Protestant Reformation, and although it was vigorously suppressed by unsympathetic Catholics more than two centuries after the order was founded, it revived again so forcefully that today the Jesuits are found the world over. In the United States, at present, their fathers number 2,400, and their scholastics, or prospective priests of collegiate grade, about 4,000. They have 279 colleges and universities and many secondary schools.[1]

HOW FAR EXTENDED

Their missionaries in early days went even as far as China and were very successful in South America and Mexico. They came up from Mexico into California, preceding the Franciscans in an attempt to take that territory for Christianity. Jesuit priests were brought to Maryland by Lord Baltimore. They sailed up the St. Lawrence River to Quebec and penetrated the howling wilderness as far as Mackinaw, where they had a famous center among the Indians. They spread southward over western New York and westward to Illinois, Wisconsin, and Minnesota. Indeed, it was

[1] *The American Catholic Who's Who and Year Book*, Romig, Detroit, 1936-37.

a Jesuit missionary, Marquette, who discovered the Mississippi River. Then they extended their efforts as far south as Louisiana.

They have figured so largely in the history of our country that it is well for us to learn something about the founder of the order and the especial urge that led him to organize the movement. For behind all movements have been real demands for meeting a crisis or setting the world onward in its progress. The followers of a great man may enlarge and modify his ideas for better or for worse, but the spark that touches off the fire in the many men who follow happens first in the brain of the founder who conceives the first idea.

FOUR GREAT CATHOLIC ORDERS

Benedictines. Each of the great Catholic orders has had a primary motive for its start, a motive incited by some great need of the times as the founders saw it. The Benedictine Order, founded in the early part of the sixth century A. D. by Benedict of Nursia, Italy, was an effort to secure a quiet *retreat* away from the world's wicked influences, where young men, and later women, might be trained in holy living and in using their various talents in creative work as they could only in a place of order, peace, and holy influences.

Dominicans. The Dominicans, founded in the early part of the thirteenth century by Saint Dominic of Spain, was a preaching order. There were at the time heretics arguing and preaching their heresies loudly, in Spain especially, and winning over many of the more intellectual type of Christians. Dominic saw the need of better educated priests, more sincere in their willingness to sacrifice their own comfort, who would follow him as itinerant preachers to counteract these heresies. It was an *evangelistic* order, and the evangelists must be trained at certain centers, which became monasteries. Women also were trained in convents. Many of these women were of the more intellectual type and became teachers. Dominic has been called "the apostle of faith," ardent in his endeavor to clear up all questions as to reasons for the faith of the Christian.

Franciscans. Saint Francis, on the other hand, almost a contemporary of Dominic, is called "the apostle of love," for he saw in Italy the great need of *serving people* who were sick and in trouble in a perfectly humble spirit as he thought Jesus did when he was on earth. Saint Francis was so filled with this spirit of brotherly love that he renounced his position as the son and heir of a wealthy merchant to live in poverty and go about doing good. Although he was not of the intellectual type, his sincerity and devotion have won him the reputation of the most Christ-like of Jesus' followers. Women, too, have Franciscan convents, and there was a third order for laymen who could not easily give up their family life and occupations.

Jesuits. When Ignatius Loyola founded the "Society of Jesus," or the Jesuits, in the sixteenth century, he viewed the world from a *soldier's* standpoint. He conceived the Church as God's army to capture the whole world for his service. The great question he mulled over for many years was how to do it. Out of his own experience as a soldier, and later as a student going to school when a grown man and diligently working his way up to a university education, he thought out a method of training his followers to capture the world for Christ. He saw before he died one of his disciples so fired with the same zeal that he traveled to India, Japan, and arrived in China. This was Saint Francis Xavier (to be definitely distinguished from Saint Francis of Assisi, who founded the Franciscan Order). Probably because the military idea dominated this order, women were not accepted.

IGNATIUS' METHOD OF TRAINING

It is for us here to consider especially the method of training that Ignatius devised and that has had such far-reaching effects. It must be clearly held in mind that the orders as they went on in history often departed from the simple teaching of their original founders. The Franciscans, for example, after St. Francis died, no longer held strictly to the rule of poverty, and in England later were far from abjuring education, for some of the most learned men of Oxford University were Franciscans. The Jesuits, too, branched out in many directions beyond Ignatius' ideas in the system they set up and the rules of life they thought proper to teach. It is the life and thought of Ignatius himself we here wish to look at.

HIS PERSONAL STORY

Ignatius was born in Spain, in the Castle of Loyola, in 1491. As a young man he became an officer in the Spanish army. That was the career taken for granted for sons of noble families. He is said to have been "quick on the dagger"[2] and when quite young to engage with pleasure in local family feuds, to have been so conscious of his importance as a soldier that when once he was bumped accidently on the street, he drew his sword and would have killed the man had he not been restrained. A young person so full of fire and petulance as that certainly needed a discipline and this he, himself, perceived a little later. With his impulsive disposition he was naturally generous and stood by his friends wholeheartedly when in trouble, and with all his hot-headedness was able to get along with people admirably, bearing no ill-will afterwards towards those with whom he had his duels. After many petty fights, he was able to show his real gallantry in a desperate situation when the troops of the Spanish king faced those of France on the borderland of the Pyrenees. When the older men counseled surrender, Ignatius stood out boldly and declared it was better to be killed than to retreat. He rallied his comrades, who withstood the onslaught for some time, but finally he was hit by a cannonball and his right leg smashed. The wounded soldier was picked up by the French, and after a couple of weeks he was sent home to his family a very sick man. The French surgeons had not done a very good job for him, and all the Spanish doctors of the neighborhood were called in, but even the best of them in that day operated like butchers, and while he suffered the pain most bravely, he came out of it at death's door. Even these surgeons set the leg badly, and to prevent its becoming shorter than the other, he chose a fearfully painful treatment for days.

HIS CONVERSION

While he was convalescing, he needed amusement and asked for some romantic story of chivalry; but alas! the house was searched in vain. Only two books could be found, a four-volume *Life of Christ* and the *Lives of the Saints*. The *Life of Christ* was well written

---

[2] Van Dyke, Paul. *Ignatius Loyola.* New York, Scribner, 1926, chapter III.

for that day and had been very popular, and the ***Lives of the Saints*** proved interesting too. As he lay in bed, his romantic temperament fixed his attention on "Our Lady," the Virgin Mary, and what chivalry would demand of him if he served a woman like that instead of indulging himself in the ways of the world. He realized that he felt happier when he was thinking those thoughts than ever before, and one night, when lying awake, he had a vision of "Our Lady with the Holy Child Jesus" and a call to a pure life in devotion to the service of Jesus. This was when he was thirty years old, and he gave himself then to this cause with such sincerity that he never swerved to the day of his death. The marks of his illness remained with him, for he was always somewhat lame, but he could walk and ride and even tramp long distances.

RESULTS

His brother was not altogether pleased with this religious turn to his purposes, and tried to lure him back to worldly pleasures. But he was determined, for he was soundly converted and threw all of his soldier's training and his rare ability as a general into Christian service as a knight of the Virgin Mary. But first he saw the necessity of his own training in a knowledge not given him by a soldier's career. So he sought a Dominican monastery and then traveled to Jerusalem as a pilgrim. But this was not enough. He knew he was uneducated and so, although a grown man thirty-three years old, he entered a boys' class at Barcelona. Applying his mind with great intensity, he progressed rapidly, until finally he could enter the University of Paris.

HIS DISCIPLES

In the course of time he proved to be the center of attention there, for in six years he had quietly gathered around him a group of ardent admirers, among them Francis Xavier, the man who became later the famous missionary to the Orient. These half dozen earnest young men took a vow to serve the Church and their fellow men—to go to Jerusalem if possible, for the crusades to Jerusalem had been very popular—but if they might not do that, they would offer themselves to the Pope for his direction. The Jerusalem journey proved impossible, but Ignatius saw so much corruption and so many infidels and heretics right around him that he conceived of a soldier's campaign or a spiritual war against evil in his own land. His followers should fight the battles of the Church with good military discipline. He therefore asked permission of the Pope to start the Society of Jesus on military principles. This request was at first refused, but finally granted. His first rule was *obedience,* and the members of the Society took the vow to labor wherever directed by the leader and the Pope.

"THE SPIRITUAL EXERCISES"

Of course, Ignatius himself was elected the first leader, or general, and by the time he died, fifteen years later, he had developed a constitution and a discipline for each member. That discipline was embodied in what he called, "The Spiritual Exercises," and it is quite a remarkable book from the pedagogical point of view. He himself had realized so deeply his deficiency in education that he was determined his followers should have schooling and mental training. He regarded schools as fundamental in his plan of capturing the world for Christ and the Church. Young boys should have a well-thought-out curriculum of education extending up into college training for young men, and the mature men who were to be their teachers must discipline their minds with "the Spiritual Exercises" before they should attempt to give them to others.

First, then, this little book was a collection of rules by which one was to concentrate his attention on Christ and what he did for mankind. The chief thing that impresses educators today is the way Ignatius hit upon some of the very principles stressed by good teachers in our era, especially the use of the imagination, to place vivid pictures before the mind and hold them there in order to impress the underlying meaning by close attention. He thought one should meditate on the actual scenes in Jesus' life, calling up the pictures and making them as realistic as possible. The scenes chosen were those considered most important in that era, such as the Temptation, the Seven Stages of the Cross, and the final Judgment. Many parts of Jesus' life were omitted which we today consider very important in giving us the all-around picture of Jesus' personality. But the method was a good one, and sound pedagogically

—the endeavor to call up the scenes and make vivid the actual life and work of Jesus.

A GRADED SYSTEM OF EDUCATION

Second, Loyola's attempt at a graded system of education showed wonderful foresight and had remarkable results. Today we take such a system for granted and think children could not progress at all if there were not such definite steps outlined from kindergarten to college and graduate school. But it was a very new thing in Loyola's day to have courses arranged systematically in relation to one another and in relation to the age of the student. There had been no systematic study of the needs of the child. Loyola himself did not outline the full system as we find it in operation later in the Jesuit schools. His disciples helped him to formulate it, but he started the idea and set his followers to thinking along that line. He had been so deprived of education as a boy and young man, and had felt the need of such training so badly when he became a man, that he was determined boys should have it as they grew up.

HIS DRILL AS A SOLDIER

He realized the power of a trained mind in capturing the world for Christ. Charlemagne had done a great deal to further education, engaging the scholar Alcuin to help him. Not only did the monasteries carry on schools at the time of Loyola, but universities had been established, such as the one in Paris that Loyola himself attended. But Loyola's drill as a soldier gave him the idea that systematic discipline of the mind was necessary if men were to be good and obedient soldiers of Christ. The Jesuit schools sprang up just when the revival of learning was spreading over Europe, and they helped it along by insisting that young men should have a *regulated* education, that they should not try to discuss philosophy and theology before they had had the preliminary studies of literature and grammar.

After ten years of reflection upon what he wanted as the fundamental principles for his followers, he presented his Constitution to them, and after his death it was presented to the Pope for his sanction. The order was confirmed by the Pope in 1540.

THE STUDIES

It had ten parts to it. The fourth was on Studies, in seventeen chapters. The fundamental idea was to give all students a minimum of learning and literary culture and then to educate the more promising and advanced students intensively and thoroughly. But even the university curriculum was full of subjects aimed at broad understanding of the culture of the world and of the languages that would aid missionaries in the countries to which they might be sent. In universities, all students were to study "humane letters, Latin, Greek, Hebrew, and such languages as Chaldaic, Arabic, and Indian, subject to the demands of necessity or utility, and logic, physics, metaphysics, moral philosophy and mathematics." Afterwards came theology, civil law, or medicine. Certainly this seems like quite a comprehensive education, with the exception of science, which of course no one knew about in that day as we do in this scientific age.

OTHER ITEMS

In addition, this outline included such topics as "the care of students," "the assistance to be given," "the location of buildings," "the means for maintaining the faculty," and one chapter on "spiritual ministration." He insisted on the protection of the health of the students, and so the life of the institution was to be regular and ordered as well as the studies. But he felt boys should be free to study and not be obliged to employ their extra time in earning a living. And, therefore, although poverty was one of the vows of the order, he sought endowments, in order to relieve the student of manual labor.

THE GROWTH OF THE IDEA

Ignatius died in 1556, and in a century and a half the growth of his idea was shown in the fact that there were 769 Jesuit colleges scattered over almost the entire world, unified into one system with a common curriculum and discipline and one head over all. In 1584, in Rome alone, there were 2,108 students, in Paris from two to three thousand. In 1627, the single Province of Paris had fourteen colleges and 13,195 students. By this time these colleges had become very attractive to the nobility, and the sons of the ruling class were being sent to them.

THE REFORMATION AND THE COUNTER-REFORMATION

This movement is sometimes called the Counter-Reformation, because the principle underneath Luther's Protestant Reformation was individual freedom, the right of each one to work out his own salvation, whereas the idea the Jesuits have always held is that there should be gathered under the banner of the Pope a world-wide army of Christian young men equipped intellectually to fight the battles of the Roman Catholic Church. And to do this there must be emphasis on both discipline of mind and discipline of body, on exercises and activities offering such discipline. These students were not to be monks giving themselves to pure contemplation, but were to go out into the world to capture others and bring them also into this organized movement. Jesus was thought of as militant King fighting for his kingdom, the Great Captain with the Pope as his representative on earth. The doctrine of free will was taught in this sense, that the student was free to lay down his own will, but once having laid it down in the Society of Jesus, he must obey implicitly each superior officer as the representative of the next higher until he reached Jesus as the Supreme Captain. For *obedience* was one of the vows of the good Jesuit soldier.

LATER DEVELOPMENTS

In this comprehensive system of education and obedience to authority there are many admirable factors, but certain interpretations crept in that Protestants cannot accept. One of these is called "mental reservation." They thought that the great end of capturing the whole world for the Church justified almost any means, and that to accomplish this, one need not express in his words all that he was working for and believed in the bottom of his heart. Protestants have thought this resulted in a kind of deception or justification of subtle politics in arriving at ends desired rather than open, frank sincerity, so that words, deeds, and inner purposes are all harmonious. This has been called "Jesuit casuistry" and is not sanctioned by Protestants because it leads to suspicion of motives behind apparent acts.

However, this grew up after Loyola's death, and Protestants and Catholics alike have much reason for admiration of Loyola himself. He was undoubtedly very sincere. One of his prayers reads, "Teach us, good Lord, to serve Thee as Thou deservest; to give and not to count the cost; to fight and not to heed the wounds; to toil and not to seek for rest; to labor and not to ask for any reward save that of knowing that we do Thy will."

For Discussion

1. What were the various motives behind the organization of Catholic Orders? What motive moved Ignatius Loyola to found the Society of Jesus, or the Jesuits? Are any such motives behind Protestant Church organizations today? Compare with the Salvation Army.
2. What was Ignatius Loyola's chief point of emphasis in his discipline of Christian soldiers? Does the word "disciples" of Jesus necessitate a "discipline"? What admirable pedagogical principle was beneath his "Spiritual Exercises"? Do we today follow it in getting acquainted with Jesus' life and teachings? If not, what way is better? Trace the effect of it in the art of his day and after. Compare Flemish art and Rubens' pictures in particular. Do the great paintings of the life of Jesus today emphasize different subjects and in a different way? If so, why?
3. Name the main ideas in Loyola's scheme of education. Do we today consider religious education as a necessary part of any all-around education? Do we think a Christian worker should have a broad cultural background? Is it necessary to be attached to the Church to be such a worker? Is one more effective if he is?
4. Is the Protestant Church dominated today by the idea of capturing the world for Christ? If so, what methods are upheld? Should we today sing hymns emphasizing soldiers and fighting? Was Loyola's idea physical fighting?
5. Study the influence of the Jesuits on American History.
6. Make an estimate of Loyola's greatness compared with other noted religious leaders.

For Further Reading

Van Dyke, Paul. *Ignatius Loyola.* New York, Scribner, 1926.

Workman, H. B. *The Evolution of the Monastic Ideal.* Epworth Press, London, 1927.

Goodier, Alban. *The Jesuits.* (See also *Benedictines, Dominicans,* Many Mansions Series.) New York, Macmillan, 1930.

Fülöp-Miller, René. *The Power and Secret of the Jesuits.* New York, Viking, 1930.

Walker, Williston. *The History of the Christian Church.* New York, Scribner, 1918.

Catholic Encyclopedia. New York, Universal Knowledge Foundation, 1912.

Encyclopedia Britannica, 14th edition. New York.

The American Catholic Who's Who and Year Book. Romig, Detroit, 1936-37.

William Ellery Channing

by

LOIS R. ROBISON
Author
Bronxville, New York

SEPARATISTS

EACH age in the long history of our world seems to have produced some outstanding group of men and women who find themselves unable to "live life as others live it." That is, they are forced, by something within themselves, to question the beliefs or the traditions or the social customs (or, occasionally, all three) with which the rest of their fellow men seem well content. They crave, and seek, change. They thirst for new knowledge, they are worshippers at the shrines of freedom. They question, probe, take apart in their ceaseless effort to see what is making the "wheels of life go round," and itch to set wheels of their own in motion.

Of such were the "Separatists," or Pilgrims, who, in 1620, set up their "separate" or own worship of God on the bleak, wintry shores of New England.

Almost three hundred years before, John Wyclif, in England, had given this separation movement its first hard push out of the set paths of orthodoxy. "You've been taking orders," said Wyclif, "from the wrong head. The Pope is not your master—he is neither your authority nor your guide. *But your Bible is.*"

Of such words had the revolutionary movement away from the Church of Rome been born. Then came Robert Browne, and he, in the last half of the sixteenth century, found that, out of the first revolution, started by Wyclif, an order of churches had grown to which he must object. He and his fellow "objectors" stood up in high places and voiced their loud objections to a Protestant Church now ruled by royalty and ridden hard by bishops. "There had been no bishops by Galilee's shore," said Browne. "Separate yourselves from all this and establish a 'company of redeemed believers, joined in a covenant.' "

And many did. Driven from England to Holland, and from thence setting forth to the new lands across the sea, the Separatists, or Pilgrims, or Congregationalists, sought and found freedom to worship "joined in a covenant."

BACKGROUND AND PREPARATION

On April 7, 1780, there was born, at Newport, R. I., a boy who was given the name of William Ellery Channing. He was to be New England's great ethical and religious leader of the future. His father was a graduate of Princeton University, a stronghold of stern Presbyterianism. There he had studied law. He had a clear and careful mind, and a keen interest in public affairs and the politics of his country. These he bequeathed to his son.

On his mother's side, the boy inherited more liberal thought. His mother's father had been graduated from Harvard back in 1747. Harvard was the great Pilgrim and Puritan dream of higher education for their sons come true. And able to "come true" because every last New England household had contributed to its establishment 12 pence, or a full peck of corn, or something else equal in value. But even in 1747 that great university had made some New Englanders uneasy in their sleep, for it was whispered about that within its halls young men were encouraged to think and talk with more freedom than the founders would have wished. (Could it be that these very uneasy sleepers were descendants of the very men and women who had dared their all—homes, work, security, and health in search of that very principle, freedom? It was the strangest of twists, in a strange world, that the very ones who had, with hardship untold, followed freedom's beckoning call should have most vigorously denied to others the same right.)

Young Channing grew—his developing mind receiving impressions from both sides. But his father died while he was yet very young—a boy of thirteen—and after that his training and education was more decidedly in the hands of his mother's people. Of his father, this son later wrote (in the, to us, somewhat stilted language of his day): "My recollections of my father are imperfect, as he died when I was thirteen years of age and I had been sent from home before that event. . . . Still, I have distinct impressions of his excellence in his social relations. . . . I well remember the *benignity* of his countenance and voice. . . . I recollect, distinctly, the great interest he took in all the political questions that agitated the country. I owed him much, and it is not my smallest obligation that his character enables me to join affectionate esteem and reverence with my instinctive gratitude."[1]

Naturally, family pressure sent him to Harvard rather than to Princeton. While in college, young Channing lived, at Cambridge, in the home of his uncle, who was at that time Chief Justice of Massachusetts. This arrangement gave him many advantages, for it helped him to meet and mingle with some of the best minds of that time and place, but at the same time it removed him from the rough and tumble, the happy give and take, of college dormitory life. And that was too bad. For William Ellery Channing was, even in his 'teens, deeply serious and even overthoughtful. He was extremely sensitive, both in his own relationships and also in the wider field of social conditions that he could glimpse through his environment. He never really learned to play. His health was always to suffer because he had never learned to temper the demands he continually made on his own mind and heart and strength.

Following his graduation, the young man accepted a position as tutor in a Virginia household. This assignment, which he held for more than a year, was to have more than one deep influence in his life. First, while there he drove himself so hard at his appointed task—usually studying until two or three in the morning, subjecting his body to rigorous hardening processes, such as sleeping on the floor and taking cold baths—that he for all time undermined his health. Never was he to be vigorous and full of "pep." Only by constant watchfulness over his health and strictest guarding of his almost feeble strength was he ever to be able to take active part in all those great issues of life with which his heart and his brain were

[1] *Channing's Memoirs*, vol. I, pp. 17-19.

tirelessly engaged. The library and the study became more and more his natural habitation.

On the other hand, the more mellow life of the South, with its softer outlook, its time for the enjoyment of natural pleasures, and the absence of commercial competition and financial worry, made Channing more receptive to the beauty all about him and more aware of the softer graces of life. It also forever turned him against "dollar chasing" and made the pursuit of wealth a matter of distaste to him.

The third great influence of the South came through his intimate contact, at first hand, with the institution of slavery as it had grown up south of the Mason-Dixon line. What he saw then, what he learned then, was to make him, later, one of the North's greatest and, at the same time, clearest-headed, abolitionists.

Back he went to Newport to regain his health and, with it, the decision to enter the ministry. After his theological training, he spent two years as Overseer at Harvard, where his passion for study and more study could be gratified. And then later, in 1803, he entered upon his ministry, at the Federal Street Church in Boston —a ministry to continue until 1842. An onlooker, that first day of June when William Ellery Channing took his vows of ordination, reported later that the one thing about the service which, all his life long, he was never able to forget was the pale, spiritual face of the young minister as he stood and read, in a voice trembling with deep emotion, the last stanza of the closing hymn:

My tongue repeats her vows,
Peace to this sacred house!
For here my friends and brethren dwell,
And since my glorious God
Makes thee his blest abode,
My soul shall ever love thee well.

UNITARIANISM

The early years of the nineteenth century were years when America in general, but New England in particular, was a veritable whirlpool of religious thinking. New ideas burst forth, most of them to die almost at once. Mental exercise more often than not took the form of theological argument. The magazines of the day teemed with religious discussion, and religious pamphlets rained down upon the upturned faces of all New England.

In the Congregational Church, all this welter of religious argument and hair-splitting and position-taking had deep consequences. The Church that had come to America, and landed on the historical Rock, was now itself splitting on the ugly rock of "doctrine." Liberals clashed with the orthodox Strict Calvinism, mild Calvinism, and no-Calvinism-at-all, and separated congregations, friends, and sometimes families. Curiously, among the first to go over, publicly, was the Old Pilgrim Church at Plymouth, which in 1800 called a "liberal" pastor.

What was this all about? Largely, the doctrine of Christ's divinity. Was Christ actually divine, of the same essence as the Father? Was he one part of a Trinity, all of whose parts were equal? And then what of original sin and man's right to be saved? Was man, through Adam's fall, born in sin? Could a little baby be damned? Were only a few to be saved? And those few chosen, from the beginning of Time, by God himself as he chose still others to be forever kept from the sight of his face? Or were these doctrines far from the truth as men's liberated minds saw it?

William Ellery Channing had known "all the doctrine." His father had strong Calvinistic leanings. But a more mellow light had come to the mind of the son. He could not find, in his Bible, grounds for believing in such a God. Nor could he find any injunctions against growth or knowledge of God and of man. More and more he found himself against all strict sectarianism—all strict definition of sect or creed. More and more did he come to dwell on what he called "the perfectibility of man"—and never on his "original sin."

In 1819, in a sermon, at the ordination of Jared Sparks, in Baltimore, Dr. Channing preached a sermon which was to become the platform of the Unitarian Movement in America. He himself refused to have this movement called "Liberalism," for, said he, *that* is an adjective that may be applied to men of all opinions. But whatever the name applied to the new and liberal movement, within one year of his epoch-making sermon, half of the Congregational Churches of Boston had withdrawn to later form together the Unitarian Association. Channing was its recognized leader and moving spirit, and that leadership is evidenced today on the asserted program of the Church, which is a statement of belief, voiced by the Unitarian General Conference in America:

> The Fatherhood of God.
> The Brotherhood of Man.
> The Leadership of Jesus.
> Salvation by Character and the
> Continued progress of Man, ***upward.***

For Channing believed that God was *One,* not three—a single, undivided personality. He preached that the core of all religion is the communion of the human soul directly with God. He felt that a fixed statement of belief (a creed) is an obstacle to growth in faith. Since the life of God is a growing life within us, then our consciousness of that life must be allowed continual free growth too. To him both the Bible and the Church were but outer expressions of inner truth, and so had no authority over the mind greater than the authority that is given to that mind as it listens to the inner voice of God speaking directly to it. Jesus, Channing taught and wrote and preached, had been *fully obedient* to the will of God. Therefore, he was the *one man* in whom we see perfectibility accomplished and made clear to us.

So clear was his teaching, so far ahead of his day many of his statements, that ministers and spiritually minded laymen still see them as the finest expression of their own conviction. Phillips Brooks was to say, years later, that "we all do preach Channing." Dr. Eliot, in his address on Channing, delivered at the unveiling of his statue in 1913, tells that when Don Pedro, Roman Catholic Emperor of Brazil, visited America in the 1870's, he asked to be taken to the tomb of Channing, saying that *"he had read all his published works*—some of them many times over!"

CHANNING ON EDUCATION

Believing and teaching, as he did, the perfectibility of man, Dr. Channing was naturally deeply interested in seeing man provided with ways and means of attaining that state. He believed in universal education. "Benevolence is short-sighted indeed, and must blame itself for failure, if it do not see in education the chief interest of the human race." That is a sentence taken from Channing. There should be no economy in education, was his cry. "Money should never be weighed against the soul of a child." (And remember, this was a new doctrine a full century ago.) Is it any wonder that eastern Massachusetts, listening, has always led in giving of its time and money to the cause of education, both public and private—that it led in providing instruction for rich and poor, for the blind and the insane? Dr. Channing cried continually the need of self-improvement. Mind! Mind! it required all one's care, said this man who less and less, after 1822, gave his impassioned pleas from the pulpit but sought more and more, from the vantage point of his writing table, to reach a larger audience. "We want great minds to be formed among us. We want the human intellect to do its utmost here." No wonder he drew around him Longfellow and Emerson, Thoreau and Hawthorne. Spirit and mind flowered together in this "little saint with the burning heart," as Van Wyck Brooks calls him in his *Flowering of New England*.

CHANNING ON SLAVERY

We said before that his life on a southern plantation as a young man had intensified Dr. Channing's hatred of slavery. It had. We find him, in writing of his memories of his father, saying, "On one subject I think of his state of mind with sorrow. His father, like most respectable merchants of that place, possessed slaves imported from Africa. They were the domestics of the family; and my father had no sensibility to the evil."

But hate slavery as he must, and did, yet William Ellery Channing had a deep knowledge of the owner's side of the question too, and in the rabid controversies that tore the Union apart, he maintained an intellectual honesty and justice on this grave matter, so close to his heart.

Here are some quotations from his spoken and written words of that period:

Man is a Person, not a Thing.

Man cannot justly be held and used as property.

To the slaveholder belongs the duty of settling upon and employing the best methods of liberation, and to no other. . . . It is of the highest importance that slavery should be succeeded by a friendly relation between master and slave; and to produce this, the latter must see in the former, his benefactor and deliverer.

The great step toward the removal of slavery is to prepare the slaves for self-support.

He truly believed that slavery ranked high among the world's greatest wrongs, particularly in its injury to the character of the employer as well as to the slave.

But when many northern Christians wanted all slave holders excommunicated from the church, making their battle-cry "No fellowship with slave holders," Dr. Channing steadfastly held to a more moderate view, and it was due to his influence, in great part, that the churches refused to be stampeded into so extreme a step.

OTHER VIEWS

Space will not permit us to go into all the splendid world of Dr. Channing's thought. His interests were as wide as his view of humanity could reach. Nothing that touched Man—and therefore touched God—was too small for his notice or too great for his hope. He set out to actively promote, by his word and pen, the social improvement of his world. Just as he saw, and told clearly, the evils of slavery, so did he show up intemperance. It might be of interest to note that of this evil he said, "Men cannot be driven into temperance. Cheerfulness is an antidote for drinking." He hated war, for he said, "Even a nation can commit murder." He wrote against the ill treatment of criminals and the grinding down of the poor and laboring classes. He held money-worshipers up to ridicule and shamed the lovers of luxury. He believed first, last, and always in the essential dignity of human nature and strongly preached that no good can ever come to society when greed and injustice and violence and bitter strife and race hatreds and social contempts are permitted to flourish.

He must have felt, of Christ and his program, as Clinton Scollard did in his "Bronze Christ" when he says:

> Love, love was the creed that he taught,
> And peace, perfect peace everywhere.
> The past that is dead is as naught,
> The present and future are fair.

He believed in the future—Men's future—and with all his soul he believed that Man could make it fair.

For Discussion

1. Do you think that such questions as those of "original sin," "infant damnation," "importance of miracles," and "salvation for the few" still stir the Christian Church? Do you believe that they should? Can you suggest several questions of importance today which you feel ought to be agitating the Church at this moment?
2. We do not, today, have slavery in America in the form that Dr. Channing fought against. But do we have any form of slavery today? Look carefully over the quotation given from Dr. Channing. Could they, with very little change, be used to help toward a solution of the slavery of poverty, child labor, unemployment? Can you make clear how each, or all, of his statements can be applied to any of our own modern "slavery" problems?
3. Do you think that Dr. Channing was wise in what he is quoted as saying about temperance? Can you recall recent history to prove it? What key to future efforts in the direction of temperance is to be found in his words?
4. Can you justify including Channing in a biography of "Creative Personalities"? On what grounds?
5. For a round-table discussion, choose, as a group, a topic from among the inside social interests of Dr. Channing (temperance, peace, exploitation of labor, need for wider educational opportunities, society's debt to the handicapped, etc.). Consider that topic, in the light of the present day, but upon the principles that you feel would have guided Dr. Channing.

For Further Reading

Eliot, Charles W. *Four American Leaders.* Boston, Beacon Press, 1906, chapter III.

Mead, Frank S. *See These Banners Go.* Indianapolis, Bobbs, Merrill, 1936, chapter II.

Brooks, Van Wyck. *The Flowering of New England.* New York, Dutton, 1938.

Articles on William Ellery Channing and on Unitarianism in standard encyclopedias.

George Fox

by

THOMAS R. KELLY
Associate Professor of Philosophy
Haverford College

GEORGE FOX, the founder of the Society of Friends, nicknamed "Quakers," was a rugged, tender-spirited, tireless prophet of apostolic Christian power. Like Paul of old, he lived a life in labors more abundant, in stripes above measure, in prisons more frequent, in death oft. Yet he lived in "a heavenly frame of mind," convinced that he knew at first hand the life of God dynamically energizing his inner soul, and he called thousands to be loyal to "that of God within them."

He was born of a weaver's family of comfortable circumstances, in the Midlands of England, in 1624—the same year in which the great Silesian mystic, Jakob Boehme, died. A serious-minded lad, Fox never passed through a period of excesses and the sowing of wild oats. But premonitions of the holiness and of the thorough dedication of a life committed to God seem to have been with him early. He suffered bitterly to see professing Christians—"professors," he called them—live so lightly and so loosely. With sureness and fineness of soul he saw that religion should go down to the very roots of men's lives, should recreate them inwardly and outwardly, and make them profoundly new, triumphant, tender, righteous, and dynamic.

So passionately did he long to find the fountainhead of such a life, so repulsed was he by the mild, easy-going religion about him, that he left home at the age of nineteen and wandered from town to town, from priest to priest, from leader to leader of repute, hoping to find someone who could help him out of the periphery into that fiery center of divine living of which he had a premonition. But he found these reputed leaders to be "hollow, empty casks," having "the form of godliness but not experiencing the power thereof." The scriptures became his closest companion, inciting him toward that life for which he longed but never leading him fully into it. Mental tension became great—even psychic abnormalities appeared during this time of stress and strain of soul.

Finally, when he was brought to utter exhaustion and despair through seeking to appease the burning God-thirst within him, moments of relief, of insight, of illumination began to come to him. Within him welled up the realization that the God who spoke through the prophets and apostles of old was still alive today, active in the world and within the depths of his own soul. He came to see that deep within every man's spirit was a holy place, where God Himself still spoke to every self-surrendered heart. He saw that men were not qualified to be ministers merely by having studied theology at a university—he had already probed the inner life of such men and had found how easy it was to have knowledge about God rather than knowledge of God's immediate life and power. Every man who knows this inner life and this living God is thereby qualified to be His minister. For the inner fountains of revelation that welled up in the prophets and apostles and writers of Scripture he found to be still open, flowing freely within himself and, potentially, within every man.

The climax of his spiritual discovery occurred when within him came the words, "There is one, even Christ Jesus, that can speak to thy condition." Therewith came complete joy and rest. His torn and troubled soul was integrated. The Christ of whom he had read in the narratives of Jesus was not dead, but living. Fox had experienced Him, alive and "warm, sweet, tender even yet." And when he heard this inner voice of the living Christ, he says, "My heart did leap for joy." Overwhelming "openings," stiflingly gigantic disclosures of the wonder and the love of God flooded him. A triumphant, released person, sure and unhesitant in the ever-renewed presence of this divine life and power within him, he saw all obstacles to the triumph of God's loving persuasion as *already overcome.* "I saw that there was an ocean of darkness and death;

but an ocean of light and love flowed over the ocean of darkness. In that I saw the infinite love of God."

We have lingered upon George Fox's inward journeys of the spirit. But an account of these journeys is needed in order to understand his outward life and wanderings. Ablaze with his great discovery of the living, continued, present experience of God, whom he found breaking in upon himself, he began his life as a wandering preacher of the Light that lighteth every man who comes into the world. In taverns and on street corners, in churchyards and in country fields, he called men to "mind that of God within them," to "come off from" dependence upon outward ceremonies and leaders and creeds and follow the monitions of what Clement of Alexandria called the inner Instructor. All places were equally holy to him. No specially consecrated ground was needed, no special church building was necessary for worship, for God dwells not in temples made with hands. Fox's excessive hostility to church buildings—which he called "steeple-houses" and which he said "struck at his life"—rested upon his deep consciousness of the holy, sacramental character of *all* places, times, and seasons. Abram may still, in any place, find his Bethel.

Fox's preaching fell upon waiting ears. An unusual ferment of "seekers" existed in the England of that day—men and women longing for a deeper, more inward, spiritual religion than they had found in the Protestant developments since the Reformation. Particularly in northwestern England, in Westmoreland and Cumberland, did Fox's early preaching bring large numbers of converts to become "children of the light." From Swarthmore Hall, at Ulverston, near the present-day shipbuilding town of Barrow-in-Furness, went out not only Fox but also bands of traveling preachers. These "Publishers of Truth" carried throughout Lancashire and Yorkshire and the north counties the message that "Christ Himself has come to lead His people." Margaret Fell, the mistress of the Hall, became known as the Mother of Quakerism. With untiring zeal she carried on correspondence, raised expense money, and aided in the development of the new movement, until Swarthmore Hall has been called the cradle of Quakerism.

But in the south, likewise, the Quaker message began to spread, in London through Francis Howgill and Edward Burrough, in

Bristol through John Audland and John Camm. When people discovered that these preachers were not seekers, but *finders,* they flocked in hundreds, and even thousands, to the Quaker movement so that, as these early Publishers of Truth wrote, their "net is likely to break with fishes."

Fox, as well as his fearless band of preachers, was soon accustomed to rebuffs, beatings, stonings, and jails. All too often this opposition was aroused by the local religious leaders, ministers, and priests. For the message of the Quaker prophets cut across the necessity of tithes, ceremonies, and established institutional requirements that gave prominence to these very priests and ministers. Moreover, Fox and his fellow preachers were bold and merciless in uncovering and denouncing all sham and show of religion that did not rest upon the fresh, immediate, living power of the Presence. They pressed ministers, in most embarrassing straightforwardness, to confess whether they preached from knowledge learned from books about God or from the fresh upspringings of the present life of God. Angered also were the ministers because, they said, the Quakers supplanted the Bible by the Light Within, which, they charged, was blasphemy, and the following of wandering, unstable lights capable of leading into all kinds of individual excesses.

Those were the troubled days of Oliver Cromwell and of the Commonwealth in England. Men who stirred great followings were easily suspected of disloyalty and plots to overthrow the government. George Fox's spirit was utterly alien to any thought of stirring up a military rebellion for the restoration of the Stuarts. There was no room in his life-center for such hatreds or bloody machinations as are involved in war. On an earlier occasion he had refused an officer's commission in the army, saying that he was living "in the virtue of that life and power that takes away the occasion for all wars." Nevertheless, in 1653, some lesser military men in his own county of Leicestershire broke up a large meeting and haled Fox before the colonel of the regiment, who decided to send Fox to London to be dealt with by Oliver Cromwell himself.

This first meeting between these two great religious figures of the seventeenth century makes a striking picture. Each was the product and expression of powerful spiritual developments of the age. Each cared for nothing so much as the realities of the religious life. Each was desperately in earnest, sincere, and looking for the renewal of spiritual depth in the lives of men. But one was in political power, entangled with the needs of maintaining that power; the other was a free soul, leader of a spiritual movement bent upon restoring the lost apostolic fervor and power to the Christian Church. Neither understood the other fully, yet each was worthy of respect.

The meeting took place in Whitehall Palace. Fox, totally unabashed in the presence of worldly greatness, entered Cromwell's presence with the words "Peace be to this house." As he had always refused to remove the hat to any official, lest its removal violate that democratic equality of all men which he felt so keenly, so he wore his hat in the presence of the ruler of England. And Cromwell's spirit was sufficiently discerning to understand the attitude of this erect, non-servile Friend. Their talk was not of politics and rebellions, but of the central realities of the religious life. Fox pointed out, as usual, that there was no substitute for the direct and living experience of the Spirit and power and light of the apostles and prophets. And to this Cromwell assented. At their parting, with tears in his eyes, the Great Protector seized Fox's hand and said, "Come again to my house, for if thou and I were but an hour a day together, we should be nearer one to the other." But although the two met later at several times, that deeper understanding on the verge of which they stood that morning was never fulfilled.

Instead, as Fox proceeded to further travels in southwest England, rioting opposition arose against his call to men to mind the Light within them. He was thrown, with two other Friends, into the terrible prison of Launceston, where they lay from winter until the next autumn. The latter part of the time was spent in the dungeon called "Doomsdale" under revolting conditions of filth too horrible to be printed here. But it became evident to the authorities in London that such excessive persecutions of Fox were only winning still more converts to the way of Friends. So at last release was granted, and Fox, undaunted in spirit, resumed his flaming traveling ministry and the establishing of meetings and groups of followers of the Light Within.

The closing years of the Commonwealth era were years of world-wide outreach for the young Society of Friends. Quakerism was planted in the West Indies and in the American colonies, even at the cost of four martyrs: three men and a woman hanged on Boston Common. Quaker messengers traveled to Holland, France, Germany, Russia, and even to the Sultan and the Pope.

But bitter days were ahead for the young movement. With the Restoration and the advent of Charles II to the throne, all movements were watched with extreme suspicion, lest revolts occur! Persecution, bitter and drastic, arose, and during the next two decades thousands of Quakers were made acquainted with prison life—to bear fruit later in exposure of prison conditions and in long-needed reform. Fox was thrust into a dungeon in Lancaster Castle and was only released after Margaret Fell stirred up a special protest to the king.

But soon after his release, a band of unbalanced religious enthusiasts, called Fifth Monarchy men, proclaimed that Christ was about to return and overthrow the earthly government of England and establish a new reign. This movement to "overthrow the government" made official nerves more jumpy than ever, and Friends were included in the general distrust that fell upon all novel religious ideas. An Act of Uniformity was followed by a Conventicle Act, making it illegal for more than four people to come together for worship in any manner not in conformity with the Church of England. Friends everywhere disobeyed the Act, continuing quietly to come together in waiting upon the Spirit in their meetings for worship. Officers sent to arrest the preachers found no one clergyman as their head and, puzzled by this democratic condition, they were forced to arrest great numbers. But if all the men were taken, the women remained to worship unperturbed. And, in one case at least, when both men and women were all taken to jail, the children gathered in regular order and carried on the meeting in silent waiting.

Soon the jails were full to bursting. Fox was arrested and was brought before three magistrates who "examined" him. When no grounds of any kind were found for charging him with a plot, the justices resorted to another expedient for imprisoning him, and thus proving their loyalty and zeal toward the new government. They called, "Bring the Book [the Bible] and put the oath of allegiance and supremacy to him." For they knew that Fox and the Friends refused to take an oath. This was not because they were literalists toward the saying, "Swear not at all," but because they found all words and all life must be truthful in Spirit-led men. Therefore, they refused to make special pledge of truthfulness, dividing times into those periods when they must tell the truth and those periods when, by implication, truth-telling could be relaxed. Of course Fox refused the oath and was put into the dungeon of Lancaster Castle and finally deprived of his citizenship, stripped of all property, pronounced an outlaw, and sentenced to indefinitely continued imprisonment.

The prison hardships in Lancaster Castle were so great that he could scarcely keep up his writing of bold and loving tracts and books with which he commonly occupied his imprisonments. Fourteen months of this treatment so weakened him that he could not walk. Then, in 1665, he was transferred by horse across England to Scarborough, where worse conditions prevailed. Smoke rolled up into his dungeon from the rooms beneath until he could scarcely breathe. And his cell was open to the sea, the driving rains from which kept him continually wet throughout the winter. Friends were forbidden to visit him, and he lived as "a man buried alive." But after nearly three years of imprisonment, a royal pardon was obtained for him, and he came out of Scarborough broken in health, stiff and rheumatic, but as bold as ever for the spread of Truth. The officers of the prison testified, "He was stiff as a tree, and pure as a bell; for we could never bow him."

Weakened in body, aged and stiff at forty-two, he returned immediately to his itinerant ministry and to the strengthening of the organization of Friends throughout England. His effectiveness was unimpaired. William Penn, a dashing young aristocrat, became convinced of the Quaker message and gave himself to a life rich in religious, literary, and political fruitfulness. Robert Barclay also, the future apologist for Quaker thought, was another important "convincement," although not directly from the ministry of Fox.

After advocating the setting up of schools for boys and girls where they might be taught "whatsoever things are useful and civil in the creation," he traveled with his religious message to Ireland. After his return from successes in Ireland occurred in a most natural and beautiful manner his marriage to Margaret Fell. Judge Fell, her husband, had long since passed away, their children were grown and married, and Margaret Fell had for years devoted herself to the service of Truth. After the two were agreed together that their marriage was grounded in the divine will, the children of Margaret Fell were consulted, then the members of Friends at Bristol, where they then chanced to be, and finally the marriage took place in a large meeting of Friends.

One might expect that a well-earned life of retirement at Swarthmore Hall should follow. But after a week together in Bristol, the two went to their several services in the Truth, and were, much of their married life, separated by the duties of religious journeys or the restraints of prison walls, but connected by constant correspondence through quaint but devoted letters.

Margaret Fox was soon in prison again—she had only been released for a time on suspended sentence—and Fox himself was desperately ill. However, upon his recovery, he succeeded in obtaining for his wife a pardon from the king. But as she was released from prison she received a letter from her husband saying that he felt he should go on a religious visit to America and that she must hasten to London "because the ship was then fitting for the voyage."

Of his journeys and hardships, illnesses and amazing recoveries, as he traveled the wildernesses of the Atlantic seaboard from Maryland to Rhode Island and south through Virginia, few words shall be written. But everywhere he went, crowds of spirit-hungry colonists flocked. His visit did much to give depth of root to the Quaker beginnings already made on this side of the water. After an absence of nearly two years, from August, 1671, to June, 1673, he was back in England and was joyfully welcomed by his wife in Bristol. As they journeyed northward toward home—if he may be said to have had a home—Fox was arrested again and thrown into prison at Worcester, from which he was released after fourteen months.

Now his active life was in large measure complete. To be sure, he was quickly off to Holland and to Germany, where small groups of Friends had sprung up. But his body was weak and his labors must be lightened. His time, when not occupied with traveling, was spent in literary work, in the writing of books, epistles to Friends and others all over the world, and tracts, which at that time were effective means for spreading his message of the Light of God in every man, to which all should be faithful.

In January, 1691, his worn body was completely spent. On the tenth of January he attended a remarkable meeting in Gracechurch Street, in London. Fox preached, then knelt in radiant prayer. After the meeting he returned to the nearby house of a Friend, saying, "Now I am clear, I am fully clear." Three days later he was gone.

William Penn's words are a fitting description of this warrior for peace and light and power and guidance: "In all things he acquitted himself like a *man,* yea a strong man, a new and a heavenly-minded man; a divine and a naturalist, *and all of God Almighty's making."*

For Discussion

1. What elements of Fox's deep search for final bed-rock reality and immediacy in religion are universal, recurring many times in many ages and in many men?
2. Is his central discovery one that is transient, fitted only to his period of history? Or is it an enduring discovery?
3. How far is his desire that the fountains of apostolic power may be reopened, a legitimate desire? Have other groups or religious leaders since the Protestant Reformation had the same desire?
4. Does his interpretation of religion represent a distinct type of religious interpretation? If so, how would you characterize it? Is his view nearer Catholicism or Protestantism?
5. Do *you* take religion and the soul's relation to God as seriously as did he? Would you want to? Would you dare to?
6. What elements in Fox's emphasis upon the Inner Light are distinctively Christian? What elements look toward an appreciation of the religious quest that is wider than Christianity?

For Further Reading

George Fox, an Autobiography. Philadelphia, Winston, 1911. An abridged edition entitled *The Journal of George Fox* in Everyman's Library, New York, Dutton, 1924.

Emmott, E. B. *A Short History of Quakerism.* London, Swarthmore Press.

Hoyland, J. S. *The Man of Fire and Steel.* London, James Clarke, 1932.

Jones, R. M. *George Fox, Seeker and Friend.* New York, Harper, 1930.

Knight, Rachel. *The Founder of Quakerism, a Psychological Study of the Mysticism of George Fox.* London, Swarthmore Press.

John Wesley

by

JOHN W. PRINCE
Pastor, Methodist Church
Clinton, Connecticut

JOHN WESLEY's long life stretched across the eighteenth century. England was at low ebb morally and spiritually. The tide had gone out, and ugly mud flats were showing along the shore of life. Lawlessness, crime, and immorality were increasing steadily. Heavy drinking was common in all classes of society, and gambling particularly in the upper circles. Government was corrupt. The churches and the clergy were on the whole lifeless, and such religion as there was could not inspire any change in conditions, so superficial was it. The masses were in deep poverty and were shamefully neglected. The poor were crying out for better things, and among the more thoughtful there was a search for something that could lead to salvation in national, church, and personal life. Nothing needed a revival so much as religion. The times were crying for a leader. The man who came upon the scene as answer to the cry was John Wesley. He was born in Epworth on June 17, 1703, and died in London on March 2, 1791. He found England in an almost hopeless state and left it wonderfully transformed.

By heredity and training he was especially fitted for a place of leadership. His father was a clergyman in the Church of England, rector of the rural parish of Epworth. His mother's religious life was one of deep warmth and vitality, and her mind original and powerful. On both his mother's and father's side there were many fearless Christian ministers. Between the years 1714 and 1720 John Wesley was a student in the Charterhouse School. In 1720 he entered Christ Church College, Oxford, where he distinguished himself as a scholar. There was little surprise when, in 1726, he was chosen Fellow of Lincoln College in the same university. His zeal and leadership in religion were recognized early in a group of students who met to aid one another in their studies and in their religious duties. In derision of the strict self-discipline and formality in religious practices of this group, people called them the "Holy Club" and later "Methodists," a nickname that was to stick. To this group of students belonged John's younger brother Charles, a student at Christ Church. He was one day to become the poet and hymn writer of the evangelical movement. Before long, George Whitefield, the man later recognized as the most powerful preacher of the eighteenth century, joined.

Some of the time between the years 1726 and 1729 John Wesley was his father's assistant, holding a curacy at Wroote, in the Epworth parish. Upon the death of their father in 1735, the two brothers sailed for the new colony of Georgia, to be missionaries to the settlers and Indians. Charles was also to serve as secretary to General Oglethorpe, founder of the colony. In 1737, they were joined there by George Whitefield. Their mission in itself was unsuccessful. It was remarkable, however, that this mission was even attempted—one of the signs that the call to win the world for Christ was again burdening the mind of the Protestant Church after a long period of neglect. The immediate cause of John Wesley's return to England was an unfortunate misunderstanding with a young lady who might otherwise have been his wife. He was not to marry until years later, and then only to make an unhappy choice. The sojourn of the brothers in Georgia was nevertheless of great and lasting benefit to themselves, for a group of Moravian missionaries so stirred them by the noble and peaceful Christian character of their lives that they longed to be like them.

After their return to England, Charles in 1736 and John in 1738, they at last found a satisfying religious experience. To Charles it came during a serious illness, to John it came a few days later, May 24, 1738, and in this manner. On the evening of that day he went unwillingly, as he admits in his *Journal,* to a "society meeting" of the Church of England in Aldersgate Street, London. There he heard a member read Luther's preface to the Commentary on Romans. "About a quarter before nine, while he [Luther] was describing the change which God works in the heart through faith in Christ, I felt my heart strangely warmed. I felt I did trust in Christ, Christ alone, for salvation; and an assurance was given me, that he had taken away my sins, even mine, and saved me from the law of sin and death." The work begun and nurtured by the Moravians in his life had come to a climax in this Anglican meeting. This experience changed his life. Although he had been Christian since childhood, it was a cold and formal and self-centered religion, and was accompanied by anxiety and introspection. This experience at last gave him that inner peace he had so long eagerly sought. With it there went a passion to influence others to a similar transformation, which had been lacking before. The two brothers were new men henceforth.

From this time on for the rest of his life, over fifty years, John Wesley had as he says, "one point in view, to promote as far as I am able, vital, practical religion, and by the grace of God, to beget, preserve, and increase the life of God in the souls of men." Worries over his own soul's condition, which had long haunted him, were now ended. Hereafter the world was to be his parish, a world full of people in misery and neglect, and without proper guidance. He had a message especially for the unprivileged, a message declaring that God is the Father of all men and that before him all are equal and can be saved. From the beginning, the religion he preached was democratic. A Christian experience was possible for the humblest and poorest of men, for miners and colliers as well as for kings and lords. Although this sounds commonplace to us, it was something new in Wesley's day. The hope and cheer it brought was like a change in atmosphere after a north wind blows.

We are not surprised that most clergymen of the Church of England should be suspicious of such a warm religion open to everybody, nor that they refused to permit Wesley to preach in their churches. But that was not to be the end; a way was to be found and it was at hand. In 1739, George Whitefield had begun preaching in the open air in the north of England. He invited Wesley to follow his example. At first Wesley hesitated because of the irregularity of the procedure. He never formally withdrew from the Church of England. It was painful to him to take steps leading to an open breach. But shortly, seeing no other way he too went out into the fields, the highways, and hedges. He could not resist the needs of the neglected. With his first sermon in the open air began the great religious revival of the eighteenth century, and Methodism was born. He continued this work for more than fifty years, traveling over much of Great Britain, preaching and directing the religious revival. Wherever he preached he organized a class meeting, which became a Methodist society. He traveled some two hundred twenty-five thousand miles during the course of his life, and preached some forty thousand sermons. But he did much more than preach. The societies he started, he visited frequently, to supervise and direct them along right lines. This personal supervision of the revival is one great reason for its success. He held conferences with his ministers and with lay helpers, training and guiding them. He maintained boarding schools chiefly for children of the Methodist societies, and conducted other numerous institutions for charity. He wrote several books and many tracts on burning questions of the day, such as slavery, smuggling, and war. He prepared and distributed books in inexpensive editions for the poorer people.

He carried on these labors under conditions that would have discouraged most men. Often he was opposed by ignorant mobs and persecuted by unfriendly clergymen. He traveled, usually on horseback, over bad roads and in all kinds of weather. At times he lived on bread only and slept on bare boards. It is all the more remarkable, because he was a man slight of body and small in stature and never robust. He was the greatest apostle since Saint Paul, of whom he reminds us in many ways, chiefly in his great passion to increase right living, in the length of his Christian service, and in the hardships he endured.

When Wesley died at the age of nearly eighty-eight, a new England was coming to birth. As early as the middle of the century, signs of a change for the better could already be seen in the attitude of people toward religion, and in the way they lived. By the end of the century, the change was decisive. Those most powerfully affected by the revival were to be found among the masses in industrial centers. Rough and vicious miners and colliers, without respect for God or man, were transformed into sober, law-abiding citizens.

Gradually Wesley's work had its effect upon other denominations, such as the Congregational and the Baptist. In the Church of England, which came under the influence of the revival, his emphasis on conversion, faith, and service for others won many sympathizers who were called "Evangelicals." More and more men saw the need of putting political and social wrongs right again. A new spirit of philanthropy was springing up. One social reform after another swept the land, and more were to follow after Wesley's death. The lot of the poor was made better, and lines dividing the higher and lower classes were breaking down. In 1789, a bloody revolution swept through France because of the miseries of the poor. England was far less disturbed, for a more peaceful change came to pass under the work inspired by Wesley. Here are some of the reforms he fought for: He had denounced slavery as "a scandal, not only to Christianity but to humanity," and whereas, before 1750, most people thought of the slave trade as a benefit to the nation and few thought it wrong, by 1833 it was wiped out of the British dominions. He was a ceaseless enemy of intemperance. He encouraged prison reform, and the great pioneer in this reform, John Howard, gave Wesley the credit for inspiring him to fight against evil prison conditions. It is not without reason that Wesley has been called "the first great friend of the poor." Since the days when as an Oxford student he had set up schools for the poor, he kept up an interest in needy people, especially the poor sick and the poor in prison. He spread inexpensive literature in order that those who could not afford to buy books could have some education.

His labor in behalf of the sick is especially noteworthy. During many years he devoted his leisure hours to the study of medicine, and conducted several medical dispensaries for the poor. He published five different medical treatises. The one he valued most was his own original work, called *Primitive Physick; or An Easy and Natural Method of Curing Most Diseases.* Many of his remedies were quaint and indeed primitive. Some were as likely to kill as to cure, as for instance the advice to tender and weak persons to arise at four or five o'clock in the morning. But of his compassion for the suffering there can be no doubt.

When Sunday schools came into existence, Wesley and the Methodists gave them hearty support. They spread rapidly because the revival had made it seem only right that all people should have religious instruction, poor as well as rich. The coming of the Sunday school created a new interest in education, and great credit must be given to John Wesley for this. In addition to the encouragement he gave the Sunday schools, he set up schools for children in many Methodist centers, and insisted that religion be taught in Methodist homes. In this work for children he was greatly influenced by his mother's teaching and example.

Wesley lived to see Methodism spread not only in England but to America and other lands. In America, the only religious ministry many pioneers had came from itinerant Methodists, such as Francis Asbury.

These far-reaching results are now a matter of history. What has Wesley to offer for our day? That branch of the Protestant Church that looks to him as its founder is one of the largest churches in the world. That his life and message are of continuing interest cannot be doubted—an interest not confined to his spiritual followers. There seems to be no end to the books written about him and his influence. The Christian watchwords today are religious experience, right living, and social reform. These are Wesleyan emphases. Most Christians believe that religion must be a personal experience and that the life of the individual who experiences it is changed. That is what Wesley stressed from the day he first preached in the fields of England to his last words only a short time before his death. Perhaps his greatest influence today is not in the field of theology but in matters social. When you recognize that love is the highest quality of God, and is the most important element in religion, you are forced to have a concern for the welfare of all humanity down to the "plain man" in the street. That was Wesley's teaching, and the social passion that is born of it is as legitimate in our century as in his. It is true that Wesley worked to bring about a change in society mainly by changing individuals, whereas we seek to change society as well as individuals. But this is only a logical development of his teaching that was made necessary by the coming of the machine age and all the problems it has created. When the followers of Wesley work for social change, they are extending and bringing up to date what was implied in his message. It is a fresh application of the value he placed on human personality, and of the belief that the call of Christianity is for everyone, and that all are equal before God. These beliefs lead to a new social outlook now as then, but with methods that change with the times. We feel today that we are to blame for unjust and inhuman social conditions, and must work to do away with them. Like John Brown of our own history, Wesley's body has gone the way of all flesh, but his soul goes marching on.

A SELECTED QUOTATION[1]

"He possessed . . . an indefatigable industry, a cool judgment, a command over others, a faculty of organization, a singular union of patience and moderation with an imperious ambition which marked him as a ruler of men. . . . The great body which he thus founded numbered a hundred thousand members at his death, and now counts its members in England and America by millions. But the Methodists themselves were the least result of the Methodist revival. Its action upon the Church broke the lethargy of the clergy; and the "Evangelical" movement, which found representatives like Newton and Cecil within the pale of the Establishment, made the fox-hunting parson and the absentee rector at last impossible. . . . In the nation at large appeared a new moral enthusiasm which, rigid and pedantic as it often seemed, was still healthy in its social tone, and whose power was seen in the disappearance of the profligacy which had disgraced the upper classes, and the foulness which had invested literature, ever since the Restoration. A yet nobler result of the religious revival was the steady attempt which has never ceased from that day to this, to remedy the guilt, the ignorance, the physical suffering, the social degradation of the profligate and the poor. It was not till the Wesleyan impulse had done its work that this philanthropic impulse began."

For Discussion

1. Compare social and political conditions in Great Britain and France at the time of the Wesleyan revival. Without Wesley's work was an uprising in Great Britain inevitable?
2. Why did the Methodists in America in 1938 so widely celebrate the two hundredth anniversary of Wesley's Aldersgate experience? What meaning does this experience have for our day?

---

[1] Green, J. R. *A Short History of the English People,* New York, American Book Co., 1916, pp. 738-740.

3. In view of Wesley's passion to "save souls," how do you account for his great interest in social work?
4. In what ways would it have been better if Wesley's followers could have remained in the Church of England instead of forming new denominations?

For Further Reading

Nehemiah Curnock (editor). *The Journal of the Rev. John Wesley, A.M.* Standard Edition, eight volumes, London, 1909-1916.

W. J. Townsend, H. B. Workman, and George Eayres (editors). *A New History of Methodism.* London, Hodder and Stoughton, two volumes, 1909.

Winchester, C. T. *A Life of John Wesley.* New York, Macmillan, 1906.